CHRISTMAS LESSONS

*Discover a few words of wisdom
from the first Christmas*

GREG BURDINE

COPYRIGHT

DEDICATION

This book is dedicated to my family. Christmas means so much to me because I have always enjoyed it with family.

Thanks to my mom and dad in Heaven for making my early Christmas memories so good. I am still great friends with my three siblings after many crazy Christmas holidays. Thanks Dick, Joanie and Mike. We had a great time growing up.

Thanks to Judy for spending Christmas with me more than anybody else ever. I hope we can spend many more together. Children make Christmas so much fun. So, thanks to my children Jennifer, Joshua, Jill, and Justin for being the reason I spent lots of money and many late night Christmas Eves making sure Santa arrived on time. Thanks also for allowing me to continue to enjoy every Christmas with the most wonderful grandchildren anybody could hope for. Christmas is still my favorite time of the year because of all of you.

Contents

INTRODUCTION

I LOVE CHRISTMAS time. It brings back so many wonderful memories of when I was a child with my family. I am also aware that I am making Christmas memories for my children and grandchildren.

As a pastor for several years, I have preached hundreds of messages about Christmas. It never gets old. But some topics and themes become more prominent and valuable as I've been able to study the Biblical stories of Christmas.

This book was written to help you discover some of those Christmas lessons. For many, it will be a reminder of what Christmas is really all about. Others may discover some new insights surrounding this holiday. Regardless, I hope something you read will enhance the love, peace, joy and hope you have at Christmas and throughout the year.

CHAPTER 1:

GET OLD BETTER, NOT BITTER

And there was one Anna, a prophetess, the daughter of Phanuel, of the tribe of Asher: she was of a great age, and had lived with an husband seven years from her virginity; And she was a widow of about fourscore and four years, which departed not from the temple, but served God with fastings and prayers night and day. And she coming in that instant gave thanks likewise unto the Lord, and spake of him to all them that looked for redemption in Jerusalem. And when they had performed all things according to the law of the Lord, they returned into Galilee, to their own city Nazareth. (Luke 2:36-39)

ONE OF THE great missionaries of the 19th century was David Livingstone. He spent several decades in south and central Africa. He is known as a great explorer and was the first known white person to travel across Africa. He was also a dedicated medical missionary and slave abolitionist.

David Livingstone died in present-day Zambia on May 1, 1873 from malaria and internal bleeding caused by dysentery. He took his final breaths while kneeling in prayer at his bedside. Britain wanted the body to give it a proper burial, but the African tribe, which loved Livingstone dearly, would not give his body to them. Finally they relented but cut out Livingstone's heart and put a note on the body that said, "You can have his body, but his heart belongs in Africa!" Livingstone's heart was buried under an Mvula tree near the spot where he died, now the site of the Livingstone Memorial. His embalmed body together with his journal was carried over a thousand miles to the coast, where it was returned to Britain for burial at Westminster Abbey.

You may recall the story of when Henry Morton Stanley was sent by the *New York Herald* to find Livingstone. He eventually found him with the memorable greeting, "Dr. Livingstone, I presume?" By that time, Livingstone had spent thirty years in Africa, and Stanley wanted Livingstone to go to England with him. But Livingstone refused to go. Two days later, Livingstone wrote in his diary: *"March 19, my birthday. My Jesus, my King, my Life, my all, I again dedicate my whole self to Thee. Accept me, and grant, O gracious Father, that ere the year is gone I may finish my work. In Jesus' name I ask it. Amen."* It was a year later that his servants found him dead on his knees.

David Livingstone desired to age with grace. Let's be honest. Life can be difficult. The older people live, the more problems crop up. Aches, pains, and hurts multiply. These affect people physically, relationally, emotionally, and spiritually. Some people become bitter as they age, yet others become better. Like Livingstone, Anna grew better as she grew old.

Luke wrote about Anna when Joseph and Mary brought Jesus to the temple for Mary's purification and Jesus' presentation to the Lord. Though she is seldom mentioned at Christmas, she is an interesting character in the story of Jesus' birth.

Anna was a prophetess, which means she received direct revelation from God (usually about future events) and passed it along to others. This gift tells us that Anna spoke truth. Her life represented the truth. Her name means "grace" and reminds us of Hannah in the Old Testament, whose name also means grace or gracious. Anna was the daughter of Phanuel whose name means the "face of God." Everything we know about her magnifies her Lord.

Anna was also of the tribe or family of Asher. Asher was the eighth son of Jacob and his name means "happy" or "blessed." Anna knew the blessings of God and true happiness even though her outward circumstances may have indicated otherwise. Because her life represented the truth and grace of God in Christ, her joy was made full.

The Bible says Anna "was advanced in years." There are two accepted interpretations concerning Anna's age. One is that she was over 100 years old. Jewish women in Anna's day could marry as early as the age of twelve. If this were true for Anna, she would have been nineteen when her husband died and a widow for eighty-four years. This would make her 103 years old! The other interpretation is that Anna was eighty-four. Either way, Anna was advanced in years. Yet, she did not act old. You might say she discovered the fountain of youth that is available by grace through faith in Christ. The Bible says, "How blessed is the man (or woman) who does not walk in the counsel of the wicked, nor stand in the path of sinners, nor sit in the seat of scoffers! But his delight is in the law of the LORD, and in His law, he meditates day and night. He will be like a tree firmly planted by streams of water, which yields its fruit in its season and its leaf does not wither; and in whatever he does, he prospers." (Psalm 1:1-3)

Anna "lived with her husband for seven years after her marriage, and then as a widow." The word "marriage" or "virginity" and the word "lived" in the Greek imply Anna lived life morally and with godly character. She was a light for others to see. However, Anna was not immune from trials and tribulations. She knew the grief of losing a husband and the pain it brings to the heart. Being a widow in Anna's day was devastating. She would not be able to make a livelihood and would be dependent upon God's people or remarriage to survive.

After a few years of marriage, Anna was suddenly without her husband and any means of support. But Anna was rich beyond measure and never found herself alone or forsaken! Perhaps the Apostle Paul was thinking of her when he wrote: *"Honor widows who are widows indeed... Now she who is a widow indeed, and who has been left alone, has fixed her hope on God and continues in entreaties and prayers night and day."* (1 Timothy 5:2 & 6)

How did Anna succeed under such adverse circumstances? What can we learn from her on how to age well?

Anna Learned to Abide in Christ

Luke 2:37 tells us, *"She never left the temple."* She never fell away or became faithless. She kept trusting and obeying. Anna believed and depended on God not only to supply her needs but also to use her life for Him. She lived near God's presence and talked with Him each day as she would her own husband if he were still living. Jesus Christ would later share in John 15:4 the secret Anna discovered: *"Abide in Me, and I in you. As the branch cannot bear fruit of itself unless it abides in the vine, so neither can you unless you abide in Me."* Are you abiding in Christ? What he has done for Anna, he will do for you.

Anna was a Servant

The Bible says Anna was "serving night and day." She served God and people. She remained ready for opportunities the Lord would bring her way. Like Jesus, she saw her purpose to serve, not to be served. Anna served night and day "with fastings and prayers." Notice the emphasis placed on "fastings and prayers" as a significant type of service in the eyes of God. The real battle of life is fought and won on our knees. Anna serves as an example because she was continuously seeking, asking, pleading to the Lord on behalf of others. She truly honored others more than herself.

Anna Had a Thankful Heart

Anna learned to see people and circumstances through the eyes of a merciful and gracious God. God granted her eyes to see and ears to hear. Dr. Luke says, "At that very moment she (Anna) came up and began giving thanks to God." Because she abided daily with God, she saw what only the prophet Simeon saw that day. Among all the religious leaders in the Temple, only Anna and Simeon were able to see and touch the Messiah. Anna knew this Christ child was her source of joy and happiness. Therefore, she could in everything give thanks.

Anna Was a Lifestyle Witness for Jesus

She "continued to speak of Him to all those who were looking for the redemption of Jerusalem." Anna couldn't stop talking about the baby Jesus. She sought opportunities to witness each day with those looking for the redemption of Jerusalem. Her daily prayer was for the Lord to bring across her path someone who needed to hear from the Lord – someone looking for deliverance from the penalty of sin and willing to accept the good news of Jesus Christ.

Soon after graduating from college, Jim Elliot wrote in his diary: "God, I pray Thee, light these idle sticks of my life that I may burn for Thee. Consume my life, my God, for it is Thine. I seek not a long life but a full one like You, Lord Jesus."

God answered that prayer, and at the age of 28, Jim Elliot's life was cut short by the spear of an Auca Indian as he and several other young men sought to take the gospel deep into the jungles of Ecuador. Jim understood the lines of the poet, who said, "Only one life; 'twill soon be past — Only what's done for Christ will last."

God sent Jesus into this world to redeem us. His life now gives meaning to our lives. Let us then, like Anna, dedicate ourselves to serving God. Whether old or young, may you endeavor to live for God. If God gives you the opportunity to live a long life, make sure, like Anna, you age better, not bitter.

CHAPTER 2:

GOD KEEPS HIS PROMISES

A LITTLE BOY was acting up at school. The teacher called on him and asked, "Do you remember what you promised me?" The boy said, "Yes, that I wouldn't misbehave anymore." Then the teacher asked, "And do you remember what I promised you?" The boy responded, "Yes, that if I misbehaved again, I'd be sent to the principal's office. But since I broke my promise, it's okay if you do too."

Broken promises. We've all done it. We had every good intention to keep our promise when we made it. But sometimes life is not what we expected. Sometimes it's easier to break a promise than keep it. Sometimes we make too many promises that we will never keep.

Did you know God makes promises? He has made promises to His followers.

God promised that He would forgive our sin if we confess our sin (1 John 1:9). God promised that all things would work together for good for those who love Him and are called by Him (Romans 8:28). God promised that He would walk through every valley with us (Psalm 23:4). God promised eternal life to those who believe in Jesus (John 3:16). God promised to adopt and bring into His family anyone who believes and receives Jesus as Lord and Savior (John 1:12). There are many more promises for the follower of Jesus.

Just as there are promises to the follower of Jesus, there are dozens of promises about the coming of Jesus in the Old Testament. These promises are commonly called prophesies and predicted many aspects of the life of Jesus. These prophesies would help the Jews rule out any imposters and validate the credentials of the true, authentic son of God.

Christmas reminds us that God keeps His promises. The birth of Jesus was the fulfillment of the promise of God. Though there are many prophecies about other aspects of Jesus' life and ministry, I want you to appreciate the fulfilled prophecies surrounding His birth.

Christ's Manner of Birth – Virgin

The Old Testament prophesied that: *"Therefore the Lord himself shall give you a sign; Behold, a virgin shall conceive, and bear a son, and shall call his name Immanuel."* (Isaiah 7:14).

The virgin birth of Jesus is a key doctrinal belief of Christianity. Two aspects of the virgin birth make it vital.

First, the Messiah is the rightful heir to the throne of David. If Jesus had been the natural son of Joseph, He would have been cut off from all right to David's throne, for Joseph was a physical descendant of Jeconiah (Coniah: see Jeremiah 22:24-30).

Because of his sin, King Jeconiah was cursed so that none of His descendants could ever become King of the Jews. Joseph was a descendant of David through Jeconiah (Matthew 1:1, 11). But we discover in Luke 2:31, that Mary was also a descendant of David, but not through Jeconiah. Rather than ancestry from David's son, Solomon, her ancestry was from David's son, Nathan. Jesus inherited the throne from his adopted father, Joseph, but was a physical descendant from David through Mary. Had he not been virgin born, he would not have been able to be a king of Jews.

Second, there is a connection between the virgin birth and Jesus' blood. The blood flowing in an unborn baby's arteries and veins is not given to it by its mother. Life and blood are produced after the male seed enters the female egg. The first thing to appear is blood. Not one drop of blood needs to be given from the mother to the developing baby. The mother gives food, oxygen, and other life-giving nutrients, but the baby is protected from the mother's blood. God created woman so that no blood would be able to pass from her to her offspring. So why is this important to the virgin birth? Jesus could not have received any blood from His mother and He had no earthly father. Where did He get His blood? Jesus received His blood from His Heavenly Father. Jesus had perfect blood. The rest of mankind has sinful blood. All are related by the blood of Adam, passed down through every father. Jesus is sinless, has perfect blood, and His shed blood is the payment for our sins.

Christ's Place of Birth – Bethlehem

The Old Testament prophesied that: *"But thou, Bethlehem Ephratah, though thou be little among the thousands of Judah, yet out of thee shall he come forth unto me that is to be ruler in Israel; whose goings forth have been from of old, from everlasting"* (Micah 5:2). We discover its fulfillment in the birth of Jesus.

In the first century, Joseph and Mary were living in Nazareth. Mary was pregnant, and Jesus was prophesied to be born in Bethlehem. Nazareth is 80 miles from Bethlehem. How would God get Mary to Bethlehem to deliver Jesus?

Augustus Caesar was ruling the Roman Empire at the time. But God was still in charge. Caesar decreed for everyone to return to their hometown for a tax census (Luke 2:1-3). God used Caesar's edict to move Mary and Joseph the 80 miles from Nazareth to Bethlehem to keep His promise. *"And Joseph also went up from Galilee, out of the city of Nazareth, into Judea, unto the city of David, which is Bethlehem"* (Luke 2:4). Caesar unknowingly played an important part in the birth of Jesus. President James Garfield called history "the unrolled scroll of prophecy."

Just as God controlled the lives surrounding the birth of Jesus, He is in charge of your life too. He will guide you and provide all you need. The government forced Joseph to make a long trip just to pay his taxes. His wife, who had to go with him, was going to have a baby at any moment. But God kept His promise and Jesus was born in Bethlehem. Like Joseph and Mary, we can live each day by faith, trusting that God is in charge, and will always keep His promises.

Christ's Ancestry – Abraham, Judah, David

God promised to Abraham: *"And I will bless them that bless thee, and curse him that curseth thee: and in thee shall all families of the earth be blessed."* (Genesis 12:3).

God promised to Judah, the son of Jacob: *"The scepter shall not depart from Judah; nor a lawgiver from between his feet, until Shiloh come; and unto him shall the gathering of the people be."* (Genesis 49:10).

God promised about David: *"Of the increase of his government and peace there shall be no end, upon the throne of David, and upon his kingdom, to order it, and to establish it with judgment and with justice from henceforth even forever. The zeal of the Lord of hosts will perform this."* (Isaiah 9:7).

God made prophesies in the Old Testament that the Messiah would be from the family of Abraham, of the tribe of Judah, and a descendant of David. We discover in Matthew 1 (Joseph's ancestry) and Luke 3 (Mary's ancestry) that Jesus descended from Abraham, Judah, and David. Some things a person can control. But no one can control their own ancestry. The only one who could control ancestry is God. That is exactly what He did for Jesus.

These are just three prophecies about Jesus' birth. There are also prophecies about Jesus' ministry (example: in Galilee — Isaiah 9:1-2), His betrayal (example: for thirty pieces of silver — Zechariah 11:12-13), His crucifixion (example: hands and feet pierced — Psalm 22:14-16), and His resurrection (example: not stay buried — Psalm 16:10) and many others. There are 48 total prophecies about the Messiah that Jesus fulfilled.

Was Jesus' fulfillment of these prophecies a coincidence? No. The odds that one person could fulfill all 48 prophecies by accident are too great.

Maybe the gospels changed their story to make Jesus fit? The Gospel story was circulated when many people knew the truth and would have objected if they wrote it wrong. Besides, why would they fabricate stories and then be willing to be put to death for someone they knew wasn't the Messiah? Besides, the Jews and Romans would have been all over the false information.

Could Jesus have made sure He fulfilled the prophecies? Some. While on the cross, He cried, "I thirst" to fulfill prophecy. He ministered in Galilee and cleansed the Temple in fulfillment of prophecy. But how did He control the fact that the Jewish leaders paid 30 pieces of silver for His betrayal, or method of execution, or the soldiers gambling for His clothes, or His legs remaining unbroken after He died. How could he arrange for His resurrection? Or when and where He was born?

Jesus fulfilled the Old Testament promises because He is God and God always keeps His promises. Christmas means God keeps His promises. If God would go to such great lengths to keep His promises concerning Jesus' birth, we can trust Him to keep all the other the promises He has made.

CHAPTER 3:

WISE MEN SEEK JESUS

Now when Jesus was born in Bethlehem of Judaea in the days of Herod the king, behold, there came wise men from the east to Jerusalem, <u>saying</u>, Where is he that is born King of the Jews? for we have seen his star in the east, and are come to worship him. When Herod the king had heard these things, he was troubled, and all Jerusalem with him. And when he had gathered all the chief priests and scribes of the people together, he demanded of them where Christ should be born. And they said unto him, In Bethlehem of Judaea: for thus it is written by the prophet, And thou Bethlehem, in the land of Juda, art not the least among the princes of Juda: for out of thee shall come a Governor, that shall rule my people Israel. Then Herod, when he had privily called the wise men, enquired of them diligently what time the star appeared. And he sent them to Bethlehem, and said, Go and search diligently for the young child; and when ye have found him, bring me word again, that I may come and worship him also. When they had heard the king, they departed; and, lo, the star, which they saw in the east, went before them, till it came and stood over where the young child was. When they saw the star, they rejoiced with exceeding great joy. And when they *were come into the house, they saw the young child with Mary his mother, and fell down, and worshipped him: and when they had opened their treasures, they presented unto him gifts; gold, and frankincense and myrrh.* (Matthew 2:1-11)

HAVE YOU EVER imagined what would have happened if there had been three wise women instead of three wise men who visited Jesus as a baby? They would have asked for directions to the stable locally instead of going to King Herod. They would have arrived on time and helped deliver the baby. They would have cleaned the stable and brought practical food for the family to eat – like a casserole.

In every manger scene are figurines of the wise men. However, the wise men probably did not come to the manger. More than likely, they came a few months to less than two years after Jesus was born. The Scripture tells us they came to a "house" rather than a stable. Yet, we often associate the wise men with the birth of Jesus.

In addition to the timing, there are a couple of other items of interest that are often confusing. Nowhere does the Scripture say there were three of them. Three gifts were given to Jesus. But we only know that there was a plurality of men.

Also, nothing says they were kings. Only the song "We Three Kings" describes them as royalty. But we do know they were wise. A great lesson to learn from the wise men is that truly wise men (and women) will seek Jesus. I hope this chapter will help you learn about the wise men, and thus, to seek after Jesus better.

Why did God reveal Jesus to the Wise men?

Who were the wise men? Very little is known about them. As mentioned above, Matthew doesn't even record how many there were. All the Bible tells us is that they came from the East to Jerusalem. It is generally accepted that the wise men were from a group of priests in Persia. Persia was once a mighty country where modern Iran and Iraq are presently located.

In the second century, a church father named Tertullian suggested that the wise men were kings because the Old Testament had predicted that kings would come to worship the Christ (Psalm 72:10-11). Tertullian also concluded that there were three kings based on the number of gifts mentioned: gold, frankincense and myrrh. In the sixth century, someone decided that their names were Melchior, Baltazar and Gaspar.

A term that is often used of the wise men is "Magi." "Magi" comes from the Greek word "magos" and is the root word from which our modern words "magician" and "magistrate" are derived. They were probably astrologers. Astrology is the study of the movements of the planets and stars as a means of determining activities on Earth. The biblical word is "divination."

The wise men, in the eyes of the Jewish people to whom Matthew wrote his Gospel, had two strikes against them:

1. They were Gentiles – Persians to be precise. The Persian empire controlled the Holy Land following the kingdom of Babylon. To the Jews, any Gentile nation was inferior to their nation.

2. They were astrologers. Astrology was expressly forbidden, on pain of death, in the Old Testament. Several Bible passages prohibit divination (Deuteronomy 4:19; 18:9-12).

Why Did God Reveal Himself to Astrologers?

The Bible does not present a specific reason God chose to reveal Himself to pagan astrologers through a star. But three reasons may be assumed.

1. The Gospel is for all nations. The fact that God personally revealed the birth of Jesus to the wise men reveals that the Gospel is for all nations. The birth of Jesus heralded the Gospel, the good news of God. This news is not just for a select few righteous people in the world. The Gospel is for all to know.

2. The wise men sought Jesus. The star that was in the sky presented a decision for the wise men. They could just admire it and do nothing. Or they could investigate it and follow it. The wise men chose to seek and follow the star. They may not have had a complete picture of who God was. But the wise men were looking for God, as best they knew how. With little to help them, they sought out Christ to worship him. God honors a spirit within a person who seeks God. We may not get everything right – but if we have a right heart, God will honor us. God reached out to the Magi, where they were, with what interested them — a Star.

This wasn't a chance Star – God had ordained it and it had been prophesied over a millennium earlier by Balaam the prophet when he said, referring to Jesus: *"I see Him, but not now; I behold Him, but not near. A Star will come out of Jacob; a sceptre will rise out of Israel."* (Numbers 24:1)

3. The Attitude of the Magi. These wise men had a number of right attitudes:

First, they obeyed the leadings of God. They were obedient to the guidance of God. They weren't too big to follow the star. They weren't just star-gazers; they put their beliefs into action. Even though they didn't know the destination, they were prepared to step out in faith. Following the leading of the Lord can be quite risky and it can be time-consuming. The Magi probably had to go from Persia to Jerusalem – a journey of a good 1,000 miles – on foot and traveling with camels. It could well have taken several months. They persevered over dangerous territory with thieves in many places.

Second, they sought Jesus for the right reasons. If tradition is correct that these men came from Persia, it is believable that they had access to Daniel's prophetic writings. Daniel lived in exile in Babylon and Persia. One of Daniel's prophecies indicates that there would be a great anointed Jewish prince who would die (Daniel 9:21-26). Another tradition is that Balaam, the prophet from Mesopotamia, was an early member of the Magi, perhaps their founder. He prophesied of a future star identified with a king of the Jews (Numbers 24:17-19). Could the magi have followed the star because they had searched the Scriptures? Regardless, they came "to worship him" (Mt. 2:2). This reveals their true motive. Worship indicates honor and praise. They had never met Jesus. But the reason they traveled so far was to worship this unknown Prince.

Third, they gave Jesus the very best that they had. They brought costly gifts to Jesus. Their three gifts indicate the value they placed on Jesus.

Gold indicated royalty and kingship. Jesus deserves offerings of value. Frankincense was an ingredient used by the priests in temple worship. It symbolized worship. It is a gift you would give to a priest. Jesus is the Great High Priest of all mankind. Myrrh was used to embalm the dead. It appears to be a thoughtless gift for a baby. But not for this baby. These wise men knew that Jesus was born to die. Jesus came to die on a cross – to bring all of us into a new relationship with God.

Fourth, they did what God asked them to do. The wise men were completely obedient to everything God desired from them. Even after visiting Jesus, they obeyed. *"Then being divinely warned in a dream that they should not return to Herod, they departed for their own country another way"* (Matthew 2:12). Rather than take the easy way home, they obeyed God and took His way. It's good they listened to God. For had Herod caught up with the wise men, he would certainly have killed them.

Why were the wise men wise?

Everybody needs wisdom. Wisdom is needed in finances, family situations, employment, life difficulties, and in every area of your life. These men were wise because of their actions. Their actions revealed their wisdom. Why were they wise?

1. They were wise men because of the Person they sought.

    Everybody's looking for something or someone. These men were looking for the Messiah. They stated to Herod, *"Where is he that is born King of the Jews? For we have seen his star in the east, and are come to worship him."* (Matthew 2:2).

    Have you found Jesus as your own personal Savior? Are you still searching for meaning in life? All you need is in Jesus.

    Even after a person receives Jesus as Savior, their life is best lived in a constant search for Jesus. It's like a person can never get enough of Him. The Apostle Paul was in constant search for a deeper knowledge of Jesus. *"That I may know him, and the power of his resurrection, and the fellowship of his sufferings, being made conformable unto his death."* (Philippians 3:10.) Wise men always seek Him.

2. They were wise men because of the perils they fought.

    These men covered vast distance and varied dangers, including the fearful King Herod. But they were willing to face every fear to find Christ. Regardless of what you face, keep following after Jesus.

3. They were wise men because of the plan they were taught.

    The wise men were from the pagan land of Persia. But it is interesting that the prophet Daniel was once in Persia. It could be that the only Scripture the Persians had was Daniel's book. If so, they might have figured out his prophecy of the timing of the coming of the Messiah in Daniel 9:25-27. According to this passage, the time between the rebuilding of Jerusalem and the Messiah would be sixty-nine weeks of years, or 483 years. This would give them an approximate date for the birth of the Messiah.

    Another prophecy in Daniel 12:3 proclaims that the *"wise shall shine as the brightness of the firmament; and they that turn many to righteousness as the stars for ever and ever."* All of this would appeal to their interest in stars and lead them to follow the divine star. They may have little Bible to go on, but they put its words into action. This made them wise.

4. They were wise men because of the presents they brought.

    As mentioned before, their gifts were representative. Gold is a very expensive metal and represents Jesus' deity. Frankincense is a very expensive perfume and represents Jesus as a Priest. Myrrh is a very expensive herb and represents Jesus as dying Savior.

What about your gifts?

1. Like gold, will you give to Jesus a gift that you hold precious?

2. Like frankincense, will you give to Jesus your true worship?

3. Like myrrh, will you give to Jesus your life, to die to yourself and live for Him every day?

A story is told from the time of World War II of a time when a little boy and his dad were driving home on Christmas Eve. They drove past rows of houses with Christmas trees and decorations in the windows. In many of the windows, the little boy noticed a star. He asked his father, "Daddy, why do some of the people have a star in the window?" His daddy said the star meant that the family had a son in the war. As they passed the last house, suddenly the little boy caught sight of the evening star in the sky. "Look, daddy, God must have a son in the war, too! He's got a star in His window." Indeed, God has a Son who went to war with sin and died to deliver us from the penalty of sin.

Chapter 4:

Don't be a Grinch at Christmas

EVERYBODY HATES THE Grinch. He stole Christmas. Many have read the book, seen the TV special, and watched the movie. Most can sing the song. When we meet someone who doesn't like Christmas, we simply call them a Grinch. But nobody wants to be a Grinch.

The book, How The Grinch Stole Christmas, was first written by Dr. Seuss in 1957. Nine years later, in 1966, the cartoon was released with Chuck Jones, an old friend of Seuss's doing the animation. Boris Karloff narrated the story and Thurl Ravenscroft, who also provided Tony the Tiger's voice in Frosted Flakes commercials, sang "You're a mean one Mr. Grinch." CBS ran the cartoon every year for 22 years.

There is no such place as "Whoville" with people whose noses are all permanently stuck up in the air and whose hair is put up in all kinds of outlandish styles. There is no green creature called the "Grinch." But there are people who behave like the grinch. They think like the grinch, believe like the grinch, and try to hurt others like the grinch. They don't live in caves at the top of high mountains. They may be your neighbor, your mailman, your brother or sister. They may be sitting next to you in church. It would be easy to spot them if they had green fur all over their body.

How do you know if you are a Grinch? In this chapter I will share five signs that will enable you to identify the grinches in your life. To do that, we will look at the original Christmas grinch. His name was Herod and his story is told in the Bible in Matthew 2.

You know you're a grinch if you get upset when others invade your territory

Now when Jesus was born in Bethlehem of Judaea in the days of Herod the king, behold, there came wise men from the east to Jerusalem, saying, Where is he that is born King of the Jews? for we have seen his star in the east, and are come to worship him. When Herod the king had heard these things, he was troubled, and all Jerusalem with him. And when he had gathered all the chief priests and scribes of the people together, he demanded of them where Christ should be born. And they said unto him, In Bethlehem of Judaea: for thus it is written by the prophet, and thou Bethlehem, in the land of Judah, art not the least among the princes of Judah: for out of thee shall come a Governor, that shall rule my people Israel. (Matthew 2:1-6)

In Dr. Seuss' story, he introduces the Grinch at the ledge outside his cave which overlooks the village of the Whos. He's there on that ledge with his arms crossed, his head slightly tilted to one side, a scowl on his face, and his foot tapping on the snow-covered ground. He is irritated because he hears music from the village below. They are blowing their horns, and whistling their whistles, and singing their songs and making such a racket that no matter how hard he tries, he cannot shut it out. He wanted nothing to do with Whoville, the Whovillers or Christmas.

There was another grinch whose territory was invaded — Herod. He had been placed in charge of the whole land of the Jews by the Emperor of Rome. He had been given the title "the king of the Jews." Not everyone was happy about Herod's role. Most of his subjects hated him. He was paranoid that he was going to lose control at any time. He killed off anyone he considered to be a threat to the throne.

Imagine Herod's reaction when wise men from the east enter his court and say: "Where is the king of the Jews?" They were invading Herod's territory with news of another king. Herod was mad! Someone had invaded his territory and was threatening to take something that belonged to him.

God's Holy Spirit wants to invade your territory. He wants to invade you with joy and peace and love. But there are certain areas of your life where you've posted "No Trespassing" signs. If He starts to walk into that territory, your defenses go up, and you get disturbed. "I'm the king of my living room!" If Jesus is not King of all, He is not king at all.

There are a lot of people who, like the grinch, have been hurt by someone. It's easier to shut off relationships than to run the risk of being hurt again. Hurts and sorrow make us want to be by ourselves. We need to get out of our cave, listen to the music and go where the people are.

You know you're a grinch if you pretend to be something that you're not

Then Herod, when he had privily called the wise men, enquired of them diligently what time the star appeared. And he sent them to Bethlehem, and said, Go and search diligently for the young child; and when ye have found him, bring me word again, that I may come and worship him also. (Matthew 2:7-8)

The Grinch knew he was hated in Whoville. But there was someone who was loved just as much as the grinch was hated — Santa Claus. Then a light came on, and that giant ear-to-ear, devilish smile covered the Grinch's face. He would go to Whoville as Santa. But rather than deliver presents, he was going to steal every present under their tree. They would not accept him the way he was. He would pretend to be something that he was not.

Herod had the same plan. When he discovered that there was someone who was threatening to invade his kingdom, he quickly called together the chief priests to find out what the Bible had to say about where this new king was to be born. The teachers told Herod that it was prophesied that the King would be born in the city of Bethlehem. He called the wise men back and told them these words: "Go, and make a careful search for the child. As soon as you find him, report to me, so that I too may go and worship Him." Herod had no desire to worship Jesus. He was only pretending to be a worshipper of Jesus to keep the wise men from learning the truth and to get what he wanted.

There are spiritual pretenders. People who pretend that everything is okay between them and God. There are other pretenders who think that, if you knew them as they really were, you would reject them just like the Grinch thought he would be rejected without his Santa suit. If you feel like you have to wear a fake ear-to-ear smile or nice clothes to be accepted and loved, you are fooling yourself. God loves you just as you are.

You know you're a grinch if you can't join others in their joy

When they had heard the king, they departed; and, lo, the star, which they saw in the east, went before them, till it came and stood over where the young child was. When they saw the star, they rejoiced with exceeding great joy. And when they were come into the house, they saw the young child with Mary his mother, and fell down, and worshipped him: and when they had opened their treasures, they presented unto him gifts; gold, and frankincense and myrrh. And being warned of God in a dream that they should not return to Herod, they departed into their own country another way. And when they were departed, behold, the angel of the Lord appeareth to Joseph in a dream, saying, Arise, and take the young child and his mother, and flee into Egypt, and be thou there until I bring thee word: for Herod will seek the young child to destroy him. When he arose, he took the young child and his mother by night, and departed into Egypt: And was there until the death of Herod: that it might be fulfilled which was spoken of the Lord by the prophet, saying, Out of Egypt have I called my son. (Matthew 2:9-15)

With his Santa suit on, the Grinch and his dog, Max, headed down the mountain into Whoville and began going from house to house retrieving all the things that Santa had left for each little boy and girl.   Instead of joy, he held onto his bitterness. He headed up the chimney with all the toys, packed them all onto his sled and carried them to the highest peak of the mountain.

Herod too was surrounded by joy and could have joined in but refused to do so. When the wise men received his message about where the Christ was to be born, they quickly headed off toward Bethlehem. They were overjoyed! Their journey was complete! They were getting ready to be introduced to the King of the Jews, the King of kings. But Herod chose to keep his distance. Bethlehem was only 5 miles away.

Herod was close and yet so far. There are others who are close to joy too whose situations you can help change. All around are people searching for joy and peace. People who are so close to joy, but not willing to take the risk of reaching out. The Grinch and Herod both were so close to joy. But since they were unwilling to join in, they decided instead to try and steal the joy of others.

You know you're a grinch if you get infuriated when your plans don't work out

Then Herod, when he saw that he was mocked of the wise men, was exceeding wroth, and sent forth, and slew all the children that were in Bethlehem, and in all the coasts thereof, from two years old and under, according to the time which he had diligently inquired of the wise men. (Matthew 2:16)

The wise men did not return to Herod but went another way. When Herod discovered that he, the trickster, had been tricked, he was furious! In his anger, Herod came up with a new plan. If he couldn't know where the one baby was, he could still make sure that he was destroyed. Children are the ones who suffer most when adults are unwilling to follow God's plan for their lives. He had all the babies in the area under two years old killed.

The Grinch had his plan too. He placed all the stuff that he had gathered from Whoville on his sled, and then whipped little Max into pulling that overloaded sleigh to the highest cliff of the mountain. He was going to throw everything over the cliff to be destroyed on the rocks below. But his plan didn't quite work out the way he thought either.

You know you're a grinch if your heart has never been changed

Then was fulfilled that which was spoken by Jeremiah the prophet, saying, in Rama was there a voice heard, lamentation, and weeping, and great mourning, Rachel weeping for her children, and would not be comforted, because they are not. (Matthew 2:17-18)

By the time that little Max was able to reach the top of the mountain with the sleigh, it was Christmas morning. The Grinch paused to listen to what was going on down in Whoville. He knew that Cindy Lu and all the Whovillers would be waking up soon and would be rushing to their trees to open their presents. But all that they would find would be a few pieces of torn wrapping paper, or maybe an ornament or two. He expected to hear the sound of crying from Whoville. But to his surprise, instead of the sound of crying, he heard the sound of singing. And then he understood. It was at this moment in the story that the size of his heart increased. According to Dr. Seuss, "in Whoville they say — that the Grinch's small heart grew three sizes that day." The joy of Christmas comes not from the presents, the decorations, the food or anything else on the outside. It comes from something that is on the inside.

Unlike the Grinch, Herod awoke that Christmas morning to the sound of weeping. Hundreds of mothers weeping, not because their children's presents had been stolen, but because their children had been killed. We know how the story ended for Dr. Seuss' Grinch. He became a part of Whoville. He didn't need to pretend anymore. He joined them in their joy, carving the roast beast himself. He joined in the celebration. And all of that happened because his heart was changed. He wasn't a grinch anymore. He was a Who. That's where the similarity between the two stories ends. Herod's story has a different ending. Herod's heart was never changed. He died a year later. This was his chance, but he missed it. He remained a grinch forever.

Thirty Years Later

Some 30 years later, a grown Jesus stood before another Herod (You can read the story in Luke 23:6-12). This Herod was the son of the Herod of Jesus' childhood. He too was so close to the One who could have provided joy and peace for him. But, like his father, he turned out to be a grinch. He had Jesus beaten and mocked and then returned Him to Pilate to be crucified. He, like his father, received no joy from being in the presence of Jesus because he was not willing to have his heart changed. He too remained a grinch to the day of his death.

Are you a grinch? Has your heart ever been changed? The Grinch's heart was changed by what he heard. God offers to change your heart. You don't have the ability to change your own heart. It is the blood that Jesus shed on the cross for you that can take your sin away and can take your bitterness away. Let God change your heart today.

Do you know any grinches? How do you respond to them? Do you stay as far away from them as possible, like the residents of Whoville did? Or do you see beyond the green skin and reach out to them in love like Cindy Lu did? You probably know some grinches at your job, in your neighborhood, or in your family. Reach out to them and let them see the joy of Christ shining through your life. Who knows what impossibly hard heart just might be changed?

CHAPTER 5:

CHRISTMAS IS A GOOD TIME FOR JOY

I F THERE IS a single word that describes what Christmas is all about, it's the little word "joy." Several of our favorite carols mention it: "Joy to the world, the Lord is come," "O come all ye faithful, joyful and triumphant," "Shepherds, why this jubilee, why your joyous strains prolong?" "Good Christian men, rejoice, with heart and soul and voice," "Joyful all ye nations rise, join the triumph of the skies, with th' angelic host proclaim, 'Christ is born in Bethlehem.'"

I wonder how many really feel joyful at Christmas? It's not always easy to feel joyful. Part of our problem is that we've got the wrong idea about joy. We tend to connect it with happiness and think that joy depends on our circumstances.

Where does Christmas joy come from? If you are looking for Christmas joy, I suggest that you can find all you need in the story of the visit of the angels to proclaim the message of the birth of Jesus to the shepherds.

And there were in the same country shepherds abiding in the field, keeping watch over their flock by night. And, lo, the angel of the Lord came upon them, and the glory of the Lord shone round about them: and they were sore afraid. And the angel said unto them, Fear not: for, behold, I bring you good tidings of great joy, which shall be to all people. (Luke 2:8-10)

Joy comes from responding correctly to good news, not just hearing good news

The angel told the shepherds that Christ was "born this day in the city of David." The city of David is not Jerusalem — it's Bethlehem, which is about 5 miles south of Jerusalem.

Bethlehem is called the "city of David" because David grew up there along with his father, Jesse, and his seven brothers. In fact, David tended sheep in the fields outside the village, just as the shepherds were doing the night the angel appeared to them.

There is one other fact you need to know. Seven hundred years earlier, the Lord had spoken through the prophet Micah (Micah 5:2) and declared that the Messiah would be born in Bethlehem.

When Micah made this prophecy, Bethlehem was a tiny, inconsequential village. Through Micah, God told the world exactly where Christ would be born. It was no secret.

It is recorded in Matthew 2 that the wise men came to Jerusalem to find out where the King was born. Even though the religious leaders knew where the baby was to be born, and even though

Bethlehem was only 5 miles south of Jerusalem, as far as we know, not a one of them cared enough to investigate for himself. They were totally indifferent to the birth of the Messiah. They missed the most important event in world history because they couldn't be bothered.

How different the shepherds were. As good Jews, they too must have known the prophecy in Micah. When the shepherds heard from the angels the glad tidings that Christ had come, they responded by saying, "Let's go straight to Bethlehem." The theologians knew the truth but wouldn't act on it; the shepherds knew very little but what they knew, they believed and immediately acted upon.

Knowledge alone is never enough to bring true joy. Hearing the good news is wonderful. But full joy comes when we respond to the good news and discover Jesus. It's not what you know, but what you do with what you know that makes the difference.

Joy comes when we realize the miraculous life of Jesus

Let's look again at the text. The angel says, "Unto you is born this day in the city of David." Just focus on the three words — "born this day." They speak to the fact that what happened in Bethlehem was nothing less than the birth of a baby named Jesus.

There are two aspects to this truth we need to mention. The first is that there were no miracles associated with the physical birth of Jesus Christ. Even though we often speak of the virgin birth of Christ, it's important to remember that the real miracle took place nine months earlier when the Holy Spirit overshadowed Mary with the result that, although she was a virgin, she became pregnant. That was an enormous miracle which has never been repeated in the history of the world. However, from that point on, Mary's pregnancy followed the normal course of all human pregnancies leading to the momentous night in Bethlehem when she gave birth to the Lord Jesus in a stable.

Second, it's important to remind ourselves that the phrase "this day" means that it really happened. Have you heard about the "Jesus Seminar" — a group of liberal scholars who use colored pebbles to vote on whether or not the gospel stories about Jesus are true or not? Several years ago, they voted down the virgin birth of Christ. The vote was 24-1 against the biblical account of the virgin birth. People want to take the miraculous out of the Christmas story.

Voting with multi-colored pebbles, these intellectual fools decided that Mary must have had sexual intercourse, either with Joseph or some unknown man, before she became pregnant with Jesus. They also decreed the visit of the wise men a fabrication, the slaughter of the innocents a fiction, and the flight of the holy family into Egypt a fanciful allegory drawn from the Moses story in Exodus.

I mention that because Christian history has always professed its belief in the literal truth of the virgin birth. The ancient creeds put this way: "Conceived of the Holy Spirit, born of the Virgin Mary." This is one truth that has always been believed by all Christians everywhere.

So, when we read "unto you is born this day in the city of David," let us remember that it points to something true — an event that really happened. Not a legend or a myth or a nicely-told fairy tale. Everything about the story is true, including the central truth that there really was a baby born in Bethlehem who really was the Son of God.

The fact that Jesus' human life began with a miracle should give us joy to know that nothing is impossible with Him. Whatever problem or obstacle we may face can be confronted with joy because God is a God of miracles.

Joy comes because of the Purpose of the Birth of Jesus

Now we come to the climax of this verse: "a Savior, which is Christ the Lord." Here's an interesting fact that comes from the Greek text of Luke 2. When Luke wrote his account, he didn't use any articles to describe who Jesus is. It reads this way: Savior, Christ, Lord. Each word is vitally important.

He came to be <u>Savior</u>. Savior is actually an Old Testament word that means "one who delivers his people." We desperately need a Savior, don't we? When the angel announced the birth of Jesus to Joseph, he said, *"Give him the name Jesus for he will save his people from their sins"* (Matthew 1:21).

He came to be <u>Lord</u> or ruler of the universe. Lord is a term for deity. It's a synonym for God. Today he is the Lord of heaven. One day he will return and set up his kingdom on the earth. Between now and then, we Christians are called to make him

Lord of our lives on a daily basis. That means surrendering our will to Him and letting Him lead the way.

He is the <u>Christ</u>—the one sent from God. Christ is the Greek version of the Hebrew word Messiah, which means "the anointed One."

Jesus would be Savior, Lord and Christ even without His birth. But if he had never come, we would never have known it. The truth of Jesus would forever have been hidden from us.

This is the heart of Christmas. God loved us enough to send His only begotten Son. Think of it this way: He didn't send a committee. He didn't write a book. He didn't send a substitute. No, when God got ready to save the world, He sent the best that He had — His one and only Son. And in sending Jesus, He was really sending Himself. This is the stupendous truth of Christmas — Immanuel — God with us. This should bring us joy.

Joy comes when we receive Jesus personally

Our text contains one final truth for our consideration. In the King James Version, this truth comes first — "For unto you is born this day in the city of David." Pause for a moment and consider who was speaking and who was being addressed. When the shepherds heard these words from the angel, they must have been flabbergasted. We tend to overlook the fact that shepherds were near the bottom of the social order of ancient Israel. They were often poor and uneducated, and some were quite young. Not very many people would pick "shepherd" as their career path. There were many easier ways to make a living in ancient Israel.

So, when the angel says, "to you is born," he's really saying, "Christ came for lowly shepherds." But what about those religious leaders in Jerusalem who were well-respected? He came for them too, but they did not make the appropriate response.

When Christ came, His birth was first announced to the outcasts of society. They were the first ones to hear the good news of Christmas. There is a great lesson in this for all of us. Our Lord came for the forgotten people of the earth and most of the time they are the ones who receive Him with the greatest joy. Rich people often have no time for Christ, but the poor welcome Him as an honored guest.

Let me make a simple application. The angel said, "For unto you is born this day in the city of David a Savior." "Unto you." "For you." He came for you. This is where Christmas becomes intensely personal and eternally joyful. It's not enough to say abstractly that you believe Christ came. Millions of people say that and are still lost in their sins. It's not enough to say that Christ came for someone else.

You can never be saved until you say, "Christ came for me. He died for me. He rose from the dead for me." Joy to the world, the Lord is come.

Chapter 6:

God Honors the Humble

To many, Joseph is a mere footnote in biblical history. But we can be sure that God was as concerned with who would be the earthly "father" of His Son as He was of who would be His mother.

I looked in my Bible for a quote from Joseph, and to my surprise, I couldn't find one. I never thought about this before, but Joseph doesn't say a single word in the Gospels. We might assume his words are recorded, because we can imagine the conversations he had with Mary, and the Angel Gabriel. He must have talked to the innkeeper. We can visualize him teaching Jesus about carpentry. But nothing is recorded from this quiet, humble man. Except in the early life of Jesus, Mary appears alone. Although the Bible doesn't say she's a widow, we can figure that Joseph had died.

To this quiet, humble man God gave the honor of taking care of His Son. It is an encouragement to all to cultivate the attitude of humility. Scripture reminds us *"Humble yourselves in the sight of the Lord and He will lift you up"* (James 4:10). I want to focus on the aspects of Joseph's life that qualify him as an excellent role model for all people everywhere.

Joseph was a Righteous Man

Then Joseph her husband, being a just man, and not willing to make her a public example, was minded to put her away privily. (Matthew 1:19)

"Righteous" or "just" means "acting or being in conformity with divine or moral law." The strength of what we believe is measured by how much we are willing to suffer for those beliefs. Joseph was a man with strong beliefs. He was prepared to do what was right despite the pain he knew it would cause.

We are introduced to Joseph in the middle of a personal crisis. Having become engaged to a beautiful young girl, he worked hard to establish an income to support his new bride and begin a family. He is in love. He is committed to Mary. He believed she loved him, until the news that his precious bride was pregnant.

Heart-broken and betrayed, how should he respond? Should he publicly shame her? Should he turn her over to the authorities to be stoned? Her explanation of the pregnancy was unbelievable, even blasphemous. She said the child was God's child. If Mary would not have been stoned on the charge of adultery, she could have been stoned on the charge of serious blasphemy.

Joseph chose the path of mercy. Scripture records that he was "a righteous man and unwilling to put her to shame," so he "resolved to divorce her quietly." Before any divine explanation, Joseph chose mercy. No hatred. No vengeance. Certainly he could have asked a lot of questions: "How could you do this to me? Who's the father?" But, no words are recorded, only tenderness.

He would certainly be the talk of Nazareth. Friends might make snide comments. But he would not hurt Mary, no matter what he thought she had done to him. When he could have demanded a bitter sentence, he chose righteous mercy. He not only tried to do what was right, he tried to do it in the right way.

Joseph was a man of great faith

But while he thought on these things, behold, the angel of the Lord appeared unto him in a dream, saying, Joseph, thou son of David, fear not to take unto thee Mary thy wife: for that which is conceived in her is of the Holy Ghost. And she shall bring forth a son, and thou shalt call his name Jesus: for he shall save his people from their sins.... Then Joseph being raised from sleep did as the angel of the Lord had bidden him, and took unto him his wife: (Matthew 1:20-21, 24)

It is significant to note that the angel Gabriel personally appeared to Mary to inform her that she would be the mother of the promised Messiah; but "an angel of the Lord suddenly appeared to him in a dream" telling Joseph not to fear taking Mary as his wife (Matthew 1:20). It was also in a dream that an angel instructed Joseph to *"Arise, take the young Child and His mother, flee to Egypt, and stay there until I bring you word; for Herod will seek the young Child to destroy Him."* (Luke 2:13). In both instances, Joseph did not doubt, question or ponder even though it was in dreams that he saw and heard the angels' directions. Joseph, nonetheless, was obedient. He trusted God.

One night a house caught fire and a young boy was forced to flee to the roof. The father stood on the ground below with out-stretched arms, calling to his son, "Jump! I'll catch you." He knew the boy had to jump to save his life. All the boy could see, however, was flame, smoke, and blackness. As can be imagined, he was afraid to leave the roof. His father kept yelling: "Jump! I'll catch you." But the boy protested, "Daddy, I can't see you!" The father replied, "But I can see you and that's all that matters." When you can't see the future, trust the Savior.

Joseph was a man of great self-control

Then Joseph being raised from sleep did as the angel of the Lord had bidden him, and took unto him his wife: And knew her not till she had brought forth her firstborn son: and he called his name Jesus. (Matthew 1:24-25)

Out of his great respect for the miracle surrounding Mary's conception, Joseph had no sexual relationship with her until after Jesus was born. We can readily see why God chose Joseph to head the family in which His only begotten Son would be reared. He had great self-control.

Paul Harvey tells about an airline stewardess who was being ha-rassed by a slightly inebriated man up in the first-class section who was making passes at her and trying to get her to agree to meet him in his hotel suite that night. With some difficulty, she got away from him, only to encounter another man at the rear of the plane acting the same way, trying to find out where she was staying, and making suggestive proposals to her about that night. At last, the pilot announced that they were making their final approach for landing. Once again, the guy in front offered her a key to his hotel suite and begged her to meet him there. To his obvious delight, she smiled at him and accepted his key, placing it securely in the pocket of her apron. Then she worked her way back towards the rear of the plane. When she got there, she took the key out of her pocket and with a big smile handed it to the other guy and said, "Now don't be late."

It is important for us and others that we have self-control. It is the identifying mark of humility that we not indulge our selfish desires. If you find it difficult to have self-control, try yielding to the Holy Spirit's control.

Joseph was a man of humble occupation

And when he was come into his own country, he taught them in their synagogue, insomuch that they were astonished, and said, Whence hath this man this wisdom, and these mighty works? Is not this the carpenter's son? Is not his mother called Mary? and his brethren, James, and Joseph, and Simon, and Judas? (Matthew 13:54-55)

We do not know how long Joseph lived his role as Jesus' earthly father. He is last mentioned when Jesus was 12 years old. But we do know that Joseph was a carpenter and trained his son in the same trade. He picked up tools and made things. Growing up, Jesus learned a craft and worked just like the others in his community. Jesus could have grown up with another step-dad, such as a physician, priest, scholar, soldier, fisherman or shepherd or even an earthly king. But, why a carpenter?

My father-in-law was a carpenter. Several aspects of the carpenter trade were excellent priorities for Jesus. Carpenters make useful things, things that people need, like tables and chairs. The carpenter does the work and the object in his hand yields to his design. Carpenters have a plan before they build something. Carpenters work hard to take what is common and make it special. Carpenters are builders, and this is what God the Father wants us to understand about his Son — Jesus Christ is a builder. As the chosen earthly father of His Son, God dignified the person who has a humble, ordinary occupation. Joseph was a hard-worker.

Regardless of your occupation, you can serve in dignity. Others may not respect what you do. But God honors you. God honors hard work. God honors humble work that serves others.

There was one family who had some children who determined to have a puppy. Mom protested because she knew that somehow, she would end up caring for the critter. True to form, the children promised that they would take care of it. Eventually, she relented. They called the puppy, "Danny" and cared for him diligently at first. But, sure enough, as time passed, Mom found herself becoming more and more responsible for taking care of the dog. Finally, she decided that the children were not living up to their promise and she found a new home for Danny. She went to tell the children, but when she broke the news to them, she was surprised that they had almost no reaction at all. One of them even said, matter-of-factly, "We'll miss him." "I'm sure we will," mom replied, "but he is too much work for one person and since I'm the one that has to do all the work, I say he goes."

"But," protested another child, "if he wouldn't eat so much and wouldn't be so messy, couldn't we keep him?" Mom held her ground, "It's time to take Danny to his new home." Suddenly with one voice and tears in their eyes, the children exclaimed, "Danny????? We thought you said Daddy!" Don't be like this Daddy or Danny! Be like Joseph and work hard.

Joseph was a man who worshiped God

Now his parents went to Jerusalem every year at the feast of the passover. (Luke 2:41)

Joseph took his family to Jerusalem to worship. Unfavorable circumstances, a meager income, and a large family did not prevent him from seeing to it that he and his wife attended the Feast of the Passover in Jerusalem every year.

I am often surprised and saddened by the excuses that keep Christians from the church worship service. I realize that we can and should worship God privately. It's a beautiful time. But Christians are not only called to believe in Jesus, but they are called to belong to a family.

If every Christian manifested the qualities that Joseph possessed, today would be more fruitful and the church's impact for Christ in the community would be greatly enhanced. Let's accept this challenge to humbly serve God to the glory of God and allow Him to build us up.

CHAPTER 7:

JESUS IS WHAT CHRISTMAS IS ALL ABOUT

A S A SIX-YEAR-OLD first-grader I watched the first Charlie Brown Christmas over fifty years ago. I don't think I have missed a year watching this seasonal favorite. Charlie Brown can teach us a lesson about Christmas.

A Charlie Brown Christmas is the longest-running cartoon special in history, airing every year since its debut in 1965. Whimsical, melancholy, and ultimately full of wonder, for many it is not Christmas until the entire family gathers to watch the show.

A Charlie Brown Christmas features Charlie Brown's search for meaning in the Christmas holiday. His search starts by seeking to understand why he always ends up depressed around the holidays. On the advice of Lucy, he gets involved in directing a school play about the Nativity. When he loses control of the production because of the cast members' refusal to listen to him, he is given the lesser responsibility of finding a Christmas tree for the play.

Instead of buying a "big, shiny, aluminum" artificial tree as he was instructed to do by Lucy, he chooses a pitiful little twig. This makes him the target of laughter and derision by all except Linus. Charlie Brown cries out in desperation, wondering if anyone understands what Christmas is all about. Linus answers him by reciting the story of the birth of Jesus.

"And there were in the same country shepherds abiding in the field, keeping watch over their flock by night. And, lo, the angel of the Lord came upon them, and the glory of the Lord shone round about them: and they were sore afraid. And the angel said unto them, 'Fear not: for, behold, I bring you good tidings of great joy, which shall be to all people. For unto you is born this day in the city of David a Savior, which is Christ the Lord. And this shall be a sign unto you; Ye shall find the babe wrapped in swaddling clothes, lying in a manger.' And suddenly there was with the angel a multitude of the heavenly host praising God, and saying, Glory to God in the highest, and on earth peace, good will toward men."

Following the reading of Luke 2:8-14, Linus concludes his monologue by saying, "And that's what Christmas is all about, Charlie Brown."

Meanwhile, Snoopy has decorated his doghouse with colorful flashing lights and other baubles, and won 1st Prize in a decorating contest. Charlie Brown takes the decorations and puts a single ornament on his tree, which promptly collapses under the weight. He flees in despair.

Having heard Linus' explanation of what Christmas is all about, the other kids realize they've been too hard on Charlie Brown, and fix his tree up into a brilliant Christmas display using the rest of Snoopy's decorations. Charlie Brown returns to find the whole gang gathered around his tree. In a rare moment of happiness, he joins the crew in singing the Christmas carol "Hark! The Herald Angels Sing", as the closing credits roll.

A simple children's cartoon reminds us of what Christmas is all about. Charlie Brown had lost sight of the point of Christmas, until Linus shared the real meaning of Christmas. Let me share with you just a few meaningful reminders from this Scripture passage.

Christmas means God's grace has come to mankind

The first announcement of Jesus' birth was given by an angel to some anonymous shepherds. Why shepherds? Why not to priests or scribes, or even kings?

Well, King David, from whom this new king is descended, had been a shepherd most of his life. God called him from that occupation to become a shepherd over the nation of Israel.

The Messiah was to be both the Good Shepherd (John 10) and the Lamb of God sacrificed for the sins of the world (John 1:29). Perhaps these shepherds were caring for the flocks that would provide sacrifices for the temple services. It was fitting that the good news about God's Shepherd and Lamb be given first to humble shepherds.

But by visiting the shepherds, the angel revealed the grace of God. Shepherds were really outcasts in Israel. Their work not only made them ceremonially unclean, but it kept them away from the temple for weeks at a time so that they could not be made clean. They were not allowed in the city and not trusted by the general public, for often they were thieves.

God sent the first message of His Son's birth to the shepherds for a reason. Jesus would come, not to the proud and powerful, but to the outcasts, the humble, those considered "last" on the social lists. To these men God brought the first news of His Son's arrival. God does not call the rich and mighty; He calls the poor and the lowly. Even if a person is rich, they must come humbly and poor of spirit.

God still breaks into ordinary lives. Follow His instructions and praise Him for using you to accomplish His will.

Christmas means there is good news of peace for everyone

We see here the emphasis on a worldwide Gospel, not just the Jews.

What was the good news? Not that God had sent a soldier or a judge or a reformer, but that He had sent a Savior to meet man's greatest need. It was a message of peace to a world that had known much war. The famous 'Pax Romana' (Roman Peace) had been in effect since 27 BC, but the absence of war doesn't guarantee the presence of peace.

The philosopher Epictetus said, "While the emperor may give peace from war on land and sea, he is unable to give peace from passion, grief, and envy. He cannot give peace of heart for which man yearns more than even for outward peace."

The Jewish word shalom (peace) means much more than a truce in the battles of life. It means well-being, health, prosperity, security, soundness, and completeness. It has to do more with character than circumstances.

Life was difficult at that time just as it is today. Taxes were high, unemployment was high, morals were slipping lower, and a military state was in control. Roman law, Greek philosophy, and even Jewish religion could not meet the needs of the hearts of people. Then, God sent His Son!

The peace on earth referred to is the peace that only the Messiah can bring – not peace after war or conflict, but peace between sinful humanity and the holy God. Those whom God favors are those to whom He will graciously reveal His truth. The emphasis is on God – He is to be glorified, and He will bring peace to those He chooses. The entire 'good news,' brought to humanity through the birth of Jesus, came by God's decision and grace alone.

The meaning of Christmas: Good News. Good News of Salvation. Good News of Joy. Good News of Peace.

Like Charlie Brown, sometimes in the midst of all the hustle, we still ask ourselves: "Doesn't anybody know what Christmas is all about?" And when we ask that question, the answer is still what Linus spoke, as the children hushed, the music stopped, the lights went down, and the spotlight came up on that lone figure, reading those powerful words about the birth of God's own Son for the world.

Christmas means there is a gift to be discovered

Christmas is a time of giving and receiving gifts. Yet, the greatest gift a person could receive is forgiveness provided by the Savior, Jesus Christ.

The gift of forgiveness given.

I learned how to type on my mom's manual typewriter. In those days, there was no delete button. If you made a mistake, you either erased each mistake or started over with a new sheet of paper. Later I used 'White-out.' White out is a white liquid that covers over your errors, your typos, your unfortunate slip-ups. You brush on the liquid and start all over again — hopefully with no unfortunate slip-ups. Did you know that 'White-out' was invented in 1956 by Bette Nesmith Graham, the mother of Mike Nesmith of The Monkees singing group?

White Out is like forgiveness. Once applied to a wrong, it leaves behind no trace that the goof happened at all. But God's forgiveness is even better. God's forgiveness not only hides our sin. It removes our sin — just as if we had never sinned.

The angel announced to the shepherds that a gift had come — the gift of forgiveness. Every shepherd in the field had heard for a lifetime all about their sins, all about their failings, all about their need. They had made sacrifices in the temple. They had attended the feast of Israel. But deep in their hearts they knew, just as all men knew, that it wasn't enough. Though their sin had been covered by the blood of an animal, it had not been removed. Their sin had created a gulf between them and their God. And now on this night an angel shared the incredible story; it's all changing. A savior has been born to save their soul.

The gift of forgiveness opened.

Imagine Christmas morning getting up and looking at all the beautifully wrapped presents under the tree and then packing them up into a box and storing them in your basement.

Then next year you get them all out again just to look at all the beautiful wrappings. You will be thankful for how nice they look under you tree and then put them all up again for another year.

This is what many do with the Christmas story. They hear that a Savior has been born. They sing and decorate and celebrate the gift every year. But they never open the gift for themselves.

When the Shepherds heard the news that a savior had come, they went to discover the gift for themselves. Christmas is all about discovering the great gift that God brings into the world through the birth of this little baby. I hope you will open the gift of forgiveness by receiving Jesus as your personal Lord and Savior.

Christmas means family and gifts and decorations. But it also means something so much more. The Charlie Brown Christmas reminds us what it is all about.

Though I have watched A Charlie Brown Christmas many times, there is one important thing I didn't notice until recently. Right in the middle of quoting the Scripture of Jesus' birth, Linus drops his blanket. This is Linus' ever-present security blanket. Throughout the story of Peanuts, Lucy, Snoopy, Sally and others all work to no avail to separate Linus from his blanket. Even though others ridicule him, he refuses to give it up.

But in the climactic scene when Linus shares "what Christmas is all about," he drops his security blanket at the moment he utters the words, "fear not."

It is pretty clear what Charles Schultz, the creator of Peanuts, was trying to convey. The birth of Jesus separates us from our fears. The birth of Jesus separates us from the habits we are unable or unwilling to break ourselves. The birth of Jesus allows us to drop the false security we have been holding so tightly and trust and cling to Him instead. Linus encourages each of us to seek security in the only place it has always been and always will be — Jesus Christ.

CHAPTER 8:

SURRENDER TO THE WILL OF GOD

W HEN GABRIEL APPEARED to Mary, she was probably about 14 or 15 years old. She was betrothed to Joseph. The betrothal contract was solemn and as binding as marriage itself.

According to the Bible, she was a virgin. She had maintained her sexual purity, as well as her spiritual purity. She was saving herself for her husband. Mary probably had her life all planned out and things were going well.

When Gabriel made His announcement to Mary, her life was immediately turned upside down. Mary was called upon to bear shame, reproach and humiliation for the glory of God. She was to receive the greatest honor ever afforded to a woman, but at the same time it carried with it tremendous social disgrace.

Often, God allows things to happen in our life that are hard to bear and hard to understand, yet the Lord sends them our way so that we might grow in Him and come to know Him in a better way. When these times arise, it is easy to question the Lord and His judgment. It is always easy to question but it is far nobler to comply with the Lord. That is the lesson of Christmas. We must always surrender to the will of God.

Even at a young age, Mary had a godly, mature faith. She was a woman of godly character. She had certain spiritual characteristics that influenced her to fully submit to God's will.

Mary was faithful

To a virgin espoused to a man whose name was Joseph, of the house of David; and the virgin's name was Mary. (Luke 1:27)

We are told that the angel came to "a virgin." The word used refers to a female that is sexually pure. In fact, the virginity of Mary is affirmed twice in verse 27. Contrary to what liberals and others may say, the word does not simply speak of a "young woman," but it speaks of one who has never engaged in sexual intercourse. The vessel God chose to use to bring His Son into this world was a perfectly pure vessel.

Why is this important? It is important because God promised that the Savior of humanity would be "the seed of the woman," (Genesis 3:15). This simply means that God would send the Savior into the world through the body of a woman without the aid of a human male. Why? Romans 5:12 states: "Wherefore, as by one man sin entered into the world, and death by sin; and so death passed upon all men, for that all have sinned." Just as Adam passed along his human nature, he also passed along his sinful nature to his children. They inherited his sin and continued to pass it on down the line.

God's plan to send a Savior into the world involved Him sending a pure Savior, who would inherit a physical body and a human nature, but not a sinful nature. God accomplished this through the virgin birth of Jesus. *"But when the fulness of the time was come, God sent forth his Son, made of a woman, made under the law."* (Galatians 4:4)

Mary was a young woman who had been prepared for this moment. History tells us that every faithful Jewish girl was looking for the Messiah. We are also told that every Jewish girl hoped that she would be the vessel chosen through which God would send His Messiah into the world.

Mary was submissive

Mary said, Behold the handmaid of the Lord; be it unto me according to thy word. And the angel departed from her. (Luke 1:38)

Despite the shame that would come her way, despite the humiliation she would bear, Mary was willing to submit her life to the will of the Lord. By doing so, she has set an example of obedience and surrender that every child of God should follow.

When the angel appears to Mary, she is amazed and she is startled, but she is a woman prepared to respond to the will of the Lord in faith and faithfulness. Mary was ready and willing to do all the Lord asked of her.

Imagine the faith required for Mary to respond to the Lord as she did. For a young unmarried woman to become pregnant in that day was to be the focus of shame, disgrace and a possible death sentence. But Mary was willing to bear the shame and the burden of being the vessel through which God would send His Son into the world.

Thank God for people like Mary who are willing to do all the Lord requires, regardless of what it might require of them. After all, nothing reveals our love for Jesus like our unquestioning obedience to all He requests of us. *"He that hath my commandments, and keepeth them, he it is that loveth me: and he that loveth me shall be loved of my Father, and I will love him, and will manifest myself to him."* (John 14:21)

We would do well to learn to submit to God's will in every detail of our life. We need never fear the providential hand of God, for He will never do us wrong! Regardless of what might come our way in life, we can be assured that God is going to use it to get the glory and to help us learn more about Him.

Mary was godly

And Mary said, My soul doth magnify the Lord, And my spirit hath rejoiced in God my Savior. For he hath regarded the low estate of his handmaiden: for, behold, from henceforth all generations shall call me blessed. For he that is mighty hath done to me great things; and holy is his name. And his mercy is on them that fear him from generation to generation. He hath shewed strength with his arm; he hath scattered the proud in the imagination of their hearts. He hath put down the mighty from their seats, and exalted them of low degree. He hath filled the hungry with good things; and the rich he hath sent empty away. He hath helped his servant Israel, in remembrance of his mercy; As he spake to our fathers, to Abraham, and to his seed for ever. (Luke 2:46-55)

In these first few verses, Mary expresses her personal praise to the Lord for His blessings to her own life. In doing so, she sets an example that every Christian should seek to follow.

Salvation. The first object for which she lifts her voice in praise is for salvation. Like the rest of us, Mary was born in sin and stood in need of a Savior. In verse 47, she declares her dependence upon God in Heaven for salvation. She is simply praising the Lord for the salvation she possesses. Your life may be falling apart, but if you have been redeemed by the precious blood of Jesus, then you have a reason to praise the name of the Lord!

Personal Blessings. Mary knows that she does not deserve the wonderful favor of the Lord that has been extended to her. Yet, the Lord did it anyway. Mary realizes that God is doing something pretty wonderful through her life. After all, she is to be the means by which the God of eternity enters human history. While many in her day ridiculed her and talked about her, she knew that in days to come, others would look back on her obedience and know that she had been blessed by the Lord. Her reward was in the fact that God was to be glorified and that others would be blessed by her actions.

Everyone who has been saved would have to acknowledge that the Lord has done "great things" in and to us. Think of the change He made in your life. Think of the blessings you have enjoyed. Think of the benefits that are yours as a child of God.

Think of the glory that awaits out there in the future. We have been blessed abundantly! Like Mary, we all have reason to praise the name of the Lord! Are we doing it as we should?

Corporate Blessings. Mary knows that she isn't the only one who has received grace from God. His grace is to be revealed to every generation, until the return of Christ to this earth. Mary praises the Lord because He did not come to reach out to the proud and the mighty. In fact, God chose to reveal Himself to those who were poor and humble. Mary reminds us that those who realize their lack can come to the Lord and be filled, while those who think they have need of nothing can expect exactly that from God.

Faithfulness. Mary praises the Lord, not only for His blessings in her life and for His blessings upon successive generations, but she also praises the Lord for remembering to do what He has promised to do. She exalts His name because He did not forget her people, the bondage of the Jews and their longing for a Messiah. Mary praises the Lord keeping His Word! For centuries, the Jews had lived on the promise of the Lord that He would one day send a deliverer, a Messiah to redeem the people and to restore the nation to a place of righteousness and favor with God. Jesus is to be the fulfillment of those promises and Mary exalts the name of the Lord for remembering to keep His promises.

The Lord still keeps His promises. He will never allow anything He has promised to do go undone. Christian, don't ever think that God will forget about you. You are forever impressed upon His heart. He will see you through this world and into the next. He did not save you to lose you. He did not save you to forget about you. He saved you to take you home to be with Him. What a blessing!

The message of Mary's story is this: you may at times find yourself in difficult situations, but if you will surrender yourself to God and allow Him to write the script for your story, then Jesus will show up in miraculous ways. In ordinary places, in stormy places, in unpredictable places, Jesus will step into your life and change it for the better, just like He did for Mary.

With that in mind, do you have the same heart that dwelled in Mary? Are you in a personal relationship with Almighty God today? Are you in such a position in your walk with the Lord where you can truly celebrate Him at Christmas? Is there a need for you to come to Him and meet Him on a personal basis? Is there a need for you to come to Him and make some things right with Him today? Is there a need in your heart to just come and bow before Him and worship Him today? Whatever your need may be, let Him have His way in your life.

CHAPTER 9:

THE BEST THINGS HAPPEN
TO THOSE WHO WAIT

CHILDREN HAVE A hard time waiting for Christmas. Here are some actual letters that were written to Santa:

Dear Santa Claus,

When you come to my house there will be cookies for you. But if you are real hungry you can use our phone and order a pizza to go.

Dear Santa,

I want a Puppy. I want a playhouse. Thank you. I've been good most of the time. Sometimes I'm wild.

Dear Santa, (From a 4-year-old)

I'll take anything because I haven't been that good.

Dear Santa,

I'm not going to ask for a lot. Here's my list: The Etch-A-Sketch animator, 2 packs of #2 pencils, Crayola fat markers and the big gift...my own color TV! Well, maybe you could drop the pencils; I don't want to be really selfish.

Christmas is often associated with waiting.

Simeon was a man who had been looking for the appearance of the Christ for a long time. To get a sense of what he was waiting for, you need to know a little bit more about the term "Christ." Translated in the Old Testament as "Messiah," it is not so much a name (although it is used that way at times — see Acts 9:34) as it is a title expressing the work that Jesus came to accomplish. The word means "anointed."

In the Greek translation of the Old Testament it was used to refer to King Saul by David (See 2 Samuel 1:14). David was the Lord's anointed to lead Israel (See 1 Samuel 10:1). Saul was anointed with oil to be king which is symbolic of the Holy Spirit. Later he prophesied in the Spirit as evidence that the hand of God was upon him (See 1 Samuel 10:10).

"The Christ" or "the Lord's Anointed" was a title Jesus accepted for Himself (See Matthew 16:13-17; John 4:25-26). As confirmation that He was the Lord's anointed, the Father gave Him the Spirit without measure (See John 3:34). Christ was set apart to God even before He had been conceived to accomplish His Father's purposes (See Matthew 1:22-23). He offered Himself in payment for our sin (See Matthew 16:21). This was the One for whom Simeon had patiently waited... the very hope of Israel.

Following the birth of Christ, Joseph and Mary went to the temple to observe two important ceremonies in obedience to the Word of God: the presentation of the child (See Numbers

18:15-16) and the purification of the mother (See Leviticus 12:1-4, 6-7). While there, they met Simeon. Simeon's name means "one who hears and obeys." Simeon was called a "righteous and devout man." The first word indicates that he behaved well toward people. The second means that he took his religious duties seriously.

Simeon had been waiting patiently for the opportunity to see the Lord's Christ before he died because God the Holy Spirit had revealed to him that he would be given this privilege. After years of waiting, at last the moment came and hope arrived in the form of a baby. Simeon, in his sheer exuberance, offered up a prayer of thanksgiving to God and a prophecy concerning the child and his mother. In so doing, he directed our attention to three main ideas.

Christ is God's promises fulfilled

Sovereign Lord, as you have promised, you may now dismiss your servant in peace. For my eyes have seen your salvation, which you have prepared in the sight of all nations: (Luke 2:29-31).

God is the ultimate promise-keeper. He always does what He says. As a matter of fact, it is impossible for God to make a promise and not fulfill it, for that would constitute lying (1 Samuel 15:29). So here in this passage, Simeon acknowledges that God has in fact kept His word.

God kept His promise to Simeon. It had previously been revealed to Simeon by God that he would not die until He had seen the Lord's Christ (Luke 2:26). Two things are assumed, but never stated in these verses: (1) that Simeon was an old man who was drawing closer to death. (2) that Simeon had been waiting a long time for this moment. Once he had seen the fulfillment of the promise, he was ready to go. The language is that of a slave experiencing freedom for the first time. By finally setting his eyes on the Christ, Simeon was released from the burden he bore for many years waiting for His arrival.

God kept His promise to humanity (Genesis 3:15). Immediately after the fall of man, God promised to destroy the works of the Devil through the seed of the woman. The salvation that was promised long ago arrived, we are told by Simeon, in full view of all people (Luke 3:6). In other words, this didn't happen in a vacuum, but in plain sight of all who were willing to see the birth of Christ for what it was, the fulfillment of God's promise to redeem mankind.

A promise is a declaration that something specified will or will not happen. People make promises all the time, but often they amount to empty words. The following story may help you understand the impact of a promise.

After an evening out, some parents came home to the children they had left in the care of a babysitter and were pleased to find the kids all asleep. As the babysitter was about to walk out the door, she said, "By the way, I promised Tommy that if he would stay in bed, you would buy him a pony in the morning."

I'm certain there was at least one disappointed child in that home the next morning. People don't always keep promises. But when God makes a promise, He keeps it!

This was true when God promised Abraham that through Him all the peoples of the earth would be blessed (Genesis 12:3); This was true when God promised David that one of his descendants would sit on the throne forever (See 2 Samuel 7:12-13); This was true when God promised through Isaiah that Israel would be given a sign that their deliverance had arrived (Isaiah 7:14). All these promises were fulfilled in the birth of Jesus. God always keeps His promises. Simeon waited patiently for God's word to come true and then praised Him for it.

Christ is God's salvation presented

For my eyes have seen your salvation, which you have prepared in the sight of all nations: a light for revelation to the Gentiles, and the glory of your people Israel. (Luke 2:30-32)

Luke informs us that Simeon was waiting for the "consolation of Israel" (Luke 2:25). The word means "comfort by way of encouragement (Acts 9:31)." What was it that brought such comfort and encouragement so that he could say, "Now dismiss your servant in peace"? It was the message that salvation had come in Jesus. Simeon was quick to recognize that the baby boy presented in the temple by his parents was no ordinary child. He was the Christ of God who had come as "a light for revelation to the Gentiles and for glory to your people Israel."

Simeon was quick to see that Jesus came for everyone. There had never been a time when Christ was more needed than when, in God's providential timing, He came 2,000 years ago (Matthew 9:35-36). The great comfort of the Gospel is that in our present distress over the consequences of sin, Christ has come to rescue us, all of us, Jews and Gentiles alike! Jesus came to save us.

Christ is God's offer rejected

The child's father and mother marveled at what was said about him. Then Simeon blessed them and said to Mary, his mother: "This child is destined to cause the falling and rising of many in Israel, and to be a sign that will be spoken against, so that the thoughts of many hearts will be revealed. And a sword will pierce your own soul too. (See Luke 2:33-35)

Simeon transitioned from a prayer of blessing to a prophecy. In speaking to Mary, he acknowledges that while God's mighty work of salvation exalts some, it humbles others (Luke 1:34-35). Christ's impact will be one of conflict. His ultimate sacrifice, though effective for canceling the debt of sin, will become a stumbling block to Jews and foolishness to Gentiles (1 Corinthians 1:23). It will be by their response to God's offer in His son that the true motives of their hearts will be open for all to see. This conflict will reach even as far as the experience of Mary, herself.

The conflict motivated by God's offer of salvation in Christ has never really ended. To this day, we find people who have accepted it and others who have rejected it. Remember, the only sin for which a person will be sent to Hell is the rejection of Christ, God's solution for man's sin. Please don't think yourself so smart that you would miss the wonderful simplicity of the Gospel and reject God's offer.

One of the key life lessons we can learn at Christmas is patience. Sometimes the details of life cause us to become discouraged. When you feel like you are losing in life, be patient. God may have some surprises ahead of you. A story of Oklahoma football may encourage you to be patient.

In 1996, Oklahoma State University's quarterback was President Lyndon Johnson's nephew, Randy Johnson. He proved to be a mediocre quarterback for a mediocre team. But mediocre or not, he and his teammates could be lifted to legendary greatness if they managed to beat their arch rival, the University of Oklahoma, in the season-ending game. In that final game of 1996, Oklahoma State trailed late by six points. Little hope remained that they would score with almost 80 yards between them and their goal line, only minutes left on the clock, and in a steady downpour of rain. But their mud-covered uniforms didn't look half as pitiful as the sad faces of the players. As a gesture of good will, the Oklahoma State coach put in all the seniors for the last play of the game, and told Randy to call whatever play he wanted. The team huddled, and to the surprise of his teammates, Randy called play 13 — a trick play they'd never used, for the good reason that it never worked in practice. The impossible happened! Play 13 worked! Oklahoma State scored, and Randy Johnson's team won the game by one point! The fans went wild! As they carried Randy, the hero of the game, off the field, his coach called out to him, "Why in the world did you ever call play 13?" "Well, we were in the huddle," Randy answered, "and I looked over and saw old Harry with tears running down his cheeks. It was his last college game and we were losing. And I saw that big 8 on his chest. Then I look over and saw Ralph. And tears were running down his cheeks, too. And I saw that big 7 on his jersey. So in honor of those two heartbroken seniors, I added eight and seven together and called play 13!" "But Randy," the coach shouted back. "Eight and seven don't add up to 13!" Randy reflected for a moment and answered back, "You're right, coach! And if I'd been as smart as you are, we would have lost the game!"

CHAPTER 10:

GOD USES ORDINARY PEOPLE TO DO EXTRAORDINARY THINGS

CANDID CAMERA WAS an early reality show capturing people's reaction with a hidden camera. One of the episodes pulled a hoax on some of the smartest college students in America. Having put together a supposed aptitude and career assessment survey that was taken by several hundred students at one of America's Ivy League schools, the students were called in to have their results interpreted for them by an "expert." The "expert" was actually producer Allen Funt posing as the expert. A group of four young men were brought in to hear their results.

Allen Funt began by building them up: "Gentlemen, I'm honored to be in your presence. You truly excelled in this aptitude survey. Gentlemen, out of all those who took this survey, you scored way above all the rest. Gentlemen, you above all the others who have taken the survey have shown a remarkable aptitude for becoming... Shepherds!"

The reaction was hilarious: at first the guys weren't sure they had heard the "expert" right. "Shepherds?," they asked. "Did you say shepherds?" One of them asked, "Are there still people doing that stuff?" Another said, "I hate being around animals!" Another responded, "I'm allergic to wool!" Ultimately, they figured out that something wasn't quite right, and Funt had them look into the hidden camera and encouraged them to "Smile! You're on Candid Camera!"

The truth is that shepherds are not held in very high esteem in our country. We're not familiar with them at all, but our view of them is that, for the most part, they are guys who are uneducated, unsophisticated, and are probably pretty dirty, even stinky most of the time. The same low regard was also the view of the first century society. But God's thoughts are not our thoughts.

One of the wonderful Christmas lessons is that God connects with ordinary people. All through the Bible, the lowly, unpopular people are special to God. In the Christmas story, other than Mary and Joseph, the first people to see baby Jesus were the unsophisticated, uneducated, and society-shunned shepherds of Bethlehem. While the world slept on that silent night, the shepherds' lives were forever changed, and their night was anything but silent.

As you read the story of the Christmas shepherds, take their example and make your Christmas special.

The shepherds responded to the Message

And there were shepherds living out in the fields nearby, keeping watch over their flocks at night. An angel of the Lord appeared to them, and the glory of the Lord shone around them, and they were terrified. But the angel said to them, "Do not be afraid. I bring you good news that will cause great joy for all the people. Today in the town of David a Savior has been born to you; he is the Messiah, the Lord. This will be a sign to you: You will find a baby wrapped in cloths and lying in a manger." Suddenly a great company of the heavenly host appeared with the angel, praising God and saying,

"Glory to God in the highest heaven, and on earth peace to those on whom his favor rests." When the angels had left them and gone into heaven, the shepherds said to one another, "Let's go to Bethlehem and see this thing that has happened, which the Lord has told us about." So they hurried off and found Mary and Joseph, and the baby, who was lying in the manger. (Luke 2:8-16)

The angel brought "good news" (the Gospel) of "great joy" to the shepherds. But the "good news" wasn't just for them. The "good news" was not when or where the Savior was born, but rather that the Savior is born. They heard God's Word and listened. But they did more than simply listen.

The shepherds had to go see this Savior, be in His presence, and experience this peace the angel talked about. So, they came in a hurry and found their way to Mary and Joseph, and the baby as He lay in the manger.

Their urgency was the same as ours should be. They let God determine their schedule. They left the sheep and put His work ahead of their own. They stopped what they were doing and went straight to Bethlehem. They went "straight" and in "haste." It doesn't say they got other shepherds to watch their flock. They acted on faith and went where God led them. If they waited until morning, they would have missed it. Coming into town in the middle of the night was inconvenient. But they went immediately.

A pastor understood this and taught his congregation to always be flexible and ready to follow God wherever He leads. He prayed at the beginning of the morning worship service, "Lord, let something happen today that isn't in the bulletin."

Would you be as flexible as the shepherds were? If God shows you something that He wants you to do, are you ready and willing to give it the highest priority? Would you be willing to bump something off your list in order to move what it is He wants done to the top of the list? The only part of the Bible you really believe is the part that you do. They came to Jesus, and they came in a hurry.

The shepherds focused on the Gift

When the angels had left them and gone into heaven, the shepherds said to one another, "Let's go to Bethlehem and see this thing that has happened, which the Lord has told us about." So they hurried off and found Mary and Joseph, and the baby, who was lying in the manger. (Luke 2:15-16)

The focus of the shepherds was where it should be... on Jesus! Every year it seems to get harder and harder to keep things surrounding Christmas from taking over and diverting our attention away from Jesus: What kind of Christmas tree will we get? Real or artificial? Green or flocked? Icicles or no icicles on the branches? Family traditions: Who buys for who? Who shops? Who wraps? What's the menu for Christmas dinner? Even church traditions: Christmas program? Christmas caroling? Candlelight service? Nativity scene? But the shepherds got it right. They put their focus on Jesus, coming to where He was. They wanted to connect with Him.

Who did they see when they saw Jesus? He was more than a baby.

Jesus is the child of promise (Luke 2:11; Isaiah 9:2,6; Micah 9:2). The late Bible teacher, Chuck Missler, applied the modern science of probability to just eight prophecies regarding Christ. The chance that any man might have fulfilled all eight prophecies is one in ten to the seventeenth power. That would be 100,000,000,000,000,000 or one quadrillion. To get a picture of that improbability in your mind, it would be as if you were to cover the whole state of Texas with silver dollars... one hundred quadrillion of them would cover every square inch of the state and be two feet deep! Then, mark one, and only one, of those silver dollars and stir the whole mass thoroughly. Then, blindfold a man and tell him he can travel as far as he wishes, but he must pick up that one marked silver dollar alone. What chance would have of getting the right one? The same chance that prophets would have had in writing those eight prophecies and having them all come true in one man... if they had written them in their own wisdom.

Jesus is the giver of joy (Luke 2:10). Could this be why so many people are sad at Christmas. No Jesus, no joy!

Jesus is the Lamb of God (John 1:29). Shepherds were accustomed to seeing lambs meant for sacrifice. They were used to seeing lambs being cared for, watched over by people who stayed up late at night. They were familiar with the role Jesus would take on as the Shepherd of our souls.

The shepherds reported the Good News

When they had seen him, they spread the word concerning what had been told them about this child, and all who heard it were amazed at what the shepherds said to them."(Luke 2:17-18)

After seeing Jesus, the shepherds openly, publicly, and enthusiastically spoke about Jesus. They were excited to share the message of Jesus with anyone who would hear. Not all good news is shared correctly.

In December 1903, after many attempts, the Wright brothers were successful in getting their "flying machine" off the ground. Thrilled, they telegraphed this message to their sister, Katherine: "We have actually flown 120 feet. We will be home for Christmas." Katherine hurried to the editor of the local newspaper and showed him the message. The next day the headline the editor wrote as a result in his newspaper said,

"Local boys will be home for Christmas." He totally missed the big news: man had flown!

But the shepherds got it right at that first Christmas. The Bible tells us they went and "made known the saying which had been told them about this child." The "saying" from the angels was and still is profound... and the shepherds passed it along to all who would hear.

What did the angels and shepherds say? We can simplify the message in three descriptions of the baby Jesus found in Luke 2:11:

Jesus saves. *"...unto you is born this day in the city of David a Savior..."*

Jesus is the Messiah. *"... which is Christ..."*

Jesus is God. *"... the Lord."*

A familiar story relates the power of God becoming a baby. There was once a man who didn't believe in God, and he didn't hesitate to let others know how he felt about religion and religious holidays. His wife, however, did believe, and she raised their children to also have faith in God and Jesus, despite his disparaging comments. One snowy evening, his wife was taking their children to a Christmas Eve service. She asked her husband to come, but he refused. "That story is nonsense!," he exclaimed. "Why would God lower Himself to come to earth as a man? That's ridiculous!" So she and the children left, and he stayed home.

As the man looked out his window, all he saw was a blinding snowstorm. He sat down to relax before the fire that evening. Then he heard a loud thump. Something had hit the side of his house. He looked out, but couldn't see more than a few feet. When the snow let up a little, he ventured outside to see what could have been beating on his window. In the field near his house he saw a flock of wild geese. They were lost and stranded on his farm, with no food or shelter. They just flapped their wings and flew around the field in low circles, blindly and aimlessly. A couple of them had flown into his house. The man felt sorry for the geese and wanted to help them. So he walked over to the barn and opened the doors wide, then watched and waited, hoping they would notice the open barn and go inside. But the geese just fluttered around aimlessly and didn't seem to notice the barn or realize what it could mean for them.

The man tried to get their attention, but that just seemed to scare them, and they moved farther away. He went into the house and came back with some bread, broke it up, and made a bread crumb trail leading to the barn. They still didn't catch on. Now he was getting frustrated. He got behind them and tried to shoo them toward the barn, but they only got more scared and scattered in every direction except toward the barn. Nothing he did could get them to go into the barn where they would be warm and safe. He said to himself, "Why don't they follow me? Can't they see this is the only place where they can survive the storm?"

Then he thought for a moment and realized they just wouldn't follow a human. They would only understand it if he could somehow become one of them. If he could turn into a goose, they would listen to him and follow him into safety. Suddenly, he understood why Christ had come. He came to us as one of us in order to show us the way... and lead us to safety. Years of doubt vanished away, and he fell to his knees in the snow, and prayed his first prayer: "Thank You, God, for coming in human form to get me out of the storm."

Jesus was more than just a virgin-born baby, as remarkable as that fact is. Jesus is God with skin on! — He's Emmanuel, God with us. Notice what the sheperds did not report. They didn't tell any stories about frosty snowmen they saw that night... no winter wonderland talk either. Their report didn't include any talk about special decorations around the manger nor boughs of holly or beautiful candles, lights. Their message wasn't about chestnuts roasting on an open fire or sugar plums dancing in their heads. Their message wasn't about silver bells or seeing shoppers rushing home with their treasures. They didn't report anything about a little drummer boy... or jolly old St. Nick... or Father Winter... or a red-nosed reindeer.

Their report was simple. It is what is needed by ordinary people everywhere. It is what we need to be reminded of every Christmas and throughout the year. Joy has come to the world; the Lord is come. Their actions were what ours need to be. They went and told it on the mountain, over the fields, and everywhere! And their focus was where our focus needs to be this Christmas. We need to focus on Jesus.

CHAPTER 11:

CHRISTMAS IS FULL
OF SURPRISES

SOME OF MY favorite YouTube videos are of a surprise visit from a military family. Whether at a ball game, at a graduation, or a restaurant or business, these always bring a tear to my eye. But Christmas is the time of year people long to be with family. I saw one video of a soldier wrapped up in a giant Christmas present, opened on Christmas Eve. What a surprise!

But one of the greatest surprises surrounding the Christmas story is about Elizabeth and Zechariah. After years of waiting, they found out they were going to have a son.

While there is actually quite a bit of Scripture devoted to Elizabeth, she sort of gets lost in the nativity narrative. We tend to skip over her role as the mother of John the Baptist in our eagerness to magnify Mary's significance.

Elizabeth and her husband, Zechariah, lived when wicked Herod was on the throne. He was the guy who not only killed members of his own family, but also eventually ordered the extermination of all male babies under the age of two near

Bethlehem. Zechariah was a priest and Elizabeth was from a family of priests. Both of them walked with God and took their faith seriously. They lived in an unnamed village in the hill country of Judea, obscure and ordinary, yet upright before God.

As we think about Elizabeth's life, we are only given a brief glimpse of a few months in a good woman's experience. Though she had been truly blessed by God, her life seemed to be incomplete. She had no children. Though serving God, He appeared to withhold what she wanted most. But one day, she received the surprise of her life.

You can't plan for a surprise. For it would no longer be a surprise if you planned for it. But you can learn some lessons from Elizabeth.

Describe your disappointment

But they were childless because Elizabeth was not able to conceive, and they were both very old. (Luke 1:7)

As devoted as Elizabeth was, she was also deeply disappointed. Some couples today experience this kind of pain as well. In that culture, barrenness was considered to be a sign of God's disfavor, so Zechariah and Elizabeth would have lived with some shame and the knowledge that while they were devoted to God, others probably thought they had done something wrong.

It is important to understand and declare disappointments. Life is not what we want it to be and sometimes it is not what it should be. To act like everything is okay when it is not is a mistake. Though we may have unmet expectations and unanswered prayers, we also need to accept our disappointment.

Pray for God's provision

Once when Zechariah's division was on duty and he was serving as priest before God, he was chosen by lot, according to the custom of the priesthood, to go into the temple of the Lord and burn incense. And when the time for the burning of incense came, all the assembled worshipers were praying outside. Then an angel of the Lord appeared to him, standing at the right side of the altar of incense. When Zechariah saw him, he was startled and was gripped with fear. But the angel said to him: "Do not be afraid, Zechariah; your prayer has been heard. Your wife Elizabeth will bear you a son, and you are to call him John. (Luke 1:8-13)

At least once a year, Zechariah would leave home while his order served at the Temple. It was similar to being in the military reserve. This had to be difficult for Elizabeth, but she also knew that it was an honor for her husband to serve in this way. Zechariah was chosen to go into the Holy Place and burn incense. This was a once-in-a lifetime privilege and was the greatest moment in the life of any priest. As a thousand priests stand outside and thousands of worshippers have gathered in the Court of Israel, Zechariah stands alone in the holy place. Only he's not alone because an angel of the Lord suddenly appears and announces that their prayer was heard and they would have a son, John. Their prayers were answered.

This is amazing because Zechariah and Elizabeth are quite old and past the normal age to have children. It's quite possible that they had been praying for 40 years or more, but nothing had happened. Or maybe they had given up much earlier. And now they were too old. And yet here's an angel saying: "Your prayer has been heard."

There's no doubt that Zechariah and Elizabeth had an ache in their heart for many years, but they kept praying. They also kept serving and worshipping. Sometimes people get so disappointed that they end up bitter toward God and then they drop out of church. But if you unplug, you'll unravel. God often puts us in hopeless situations so we'll turn to Him. He is our only answer.

But instead of trusting God's Word, Zechariah wants some assurance that this will really happen. In Luke 1:18 he asks, *"How can I be sure of this? I am an old man and my wife is well along in years."* Because he doubted, he was given a sign, only not one he wanted. He would not be able to speak until John was born (Luke 1:20).

This is a common trait of many Christians. We pray for something and lose heart when it doesn't happen quickly. But when the answer eventually comes. we become skeptical that it is really happening. Why are we so surprised when God answers our prayers? Why do we stop praying for something because there's been no answer? Don't give up because, when you pray, God hears it.

Trust God's timing

One of the hardest things to do when we pray is to wait for God's answers. Notice God's sense of timing in Luke 1.

1:5 *"In the time of Herod..."*

1:10 *"And when the time for the burning of incense came..."*

1:20 *"...my words, which will come true at their proper time."*

1:23 *"When his time of service was completed..."*

1:24 *"After this his wife Elizabeth became pregnant and for five months remained in seclusion."*

1:26 *"In the sixth month, God sent the angel Gabriel to Nazareth..."*

1:39 *"At that time Mary got ready and hurried to a town in the hill country of Judea."*

1:57 *"When it was time for Elizabeth to have her baby, she gave birth to a son."*

When God used Gabriel to speak to Zechariah, He was breaking 400 years of silence. But the time was right for something new to be spoken. The last words in Malachi speak of the promise of a prophet who would come in the spirit of Elijah: *"Behold, I am going to send you Elijah the prophet before the coming of the great and terrible day of the Lord"* (Malachi 4:4-6).

God answers prayer according to His timing and His delays are not the same thing as His denials. God often waits until things are humanly impossible and then He does what only He can do so He can get all the glory. God waits in order to display His glory, to dispense His grace and to grow our character.

When we pray a prayer that is not right, God will say, "NO."

When we pray a prayer and we are not right, God will say, "GROW."

When we pray a prayer and the timing is not right, God will say, "SLOW."

But, when we pray a prayer and all is right, God will say, "GO."

In what area do you need to trust God's timing? Related to this, do you need to confess any anger you have toward God for not answering according to your timetable? Zechariah and Elizabeth didn't know it, but God had been planning this from the very beginning. What seemed like unexplainable silence was really God working to prepare them to be part of His plan to offer salvation to the world. Let God do His perfect work in His perfect time and stop trying to push Him to fit your imperfect schedule. Remember, before God does something new, He's working on you!

Look for ways to encourage others

The angel answered [to Mary], *"The Holy Spirit will come on you, and the power of the Most High will overshadow you. So the holy one to be born will be called the Son of God. Even*

Elizabeth your relative is going to have a child in her old age, and she who was said to be unable to conceive is in her sixth month. For no word from God will ever fail." "I am the Lord's servant," Mary answered. "May your word to me be fulfilled." Then the angel left her. At that time Mary got ready and hurried to a town in the hill country of Judea, where she entered Zechariah's home and greeted Elizabeth. When Elizabeth heard Mary's greeting, the baby leaped in her womb, and Elizabeth was filled with the Holy Spirit. In a loud voice she exclaimed: "Blessed are you among women, and blessed is the child you will bear! (Luke 1:35-42)

Elizabeth was a huge encouragement to Mary. In fact, Elizabeth's pregnancy was used as an example by the angel when he spoke to Mary. Elizabeth and Mary now had something in common because both of their pregnancies were miraculous. When they met, Elizabeth's baby leaped in her womb and then in a loud voice she praised God through Mary. Elizabeth's focus is on Mary, not on herself.

When you're going through something, look for ways that God wants to use you to encourage someone else. Most of us get so wrapped up in our own worries that we forget that there are people around us who need encouragement. In fact, one reason God ministers to us is so that we'll minister to others.

Learn from Elizabeth and look around and see who needs some encouragement today. It's likely that God wants to use you to help someone who is going through something you have already experienced.

Enjoy the blessing of believing

"But why am I so favored, that the mother of my Lord should come to me? As soon as the sound of your greeting reached my ears, the baby in my womb leaped for joy. Blessed is she who has believed that the Lord would fulfill his promises to her!" (Luke 1:43-45)

Every member of Elizabeth's family was impacted by the announcement of the Lord's salvation. Notice that Elizabeth called Jesus "my Lord" even before He was born. She then blesses Mary by affirming her for her acceptance of the Lord's will in her life. An old priest (Zechariah) had less faith than a young peasant girl (Mary). Elizabeth's blessing of Mary for her faith in God's promise contains a mild rebuke for her doubting husband, who did not believe Gabriel's words. Elizabeth seems to have had much deeper spiritual and scriptural insight than Zechariah did. She speaks of much more than she would have learned from what the angel said to her husband. She understood that not only would their son be the forerunner, but that the son of Mary is Lord and Savior. Elizabeth had no doubt that Jesus was the Lord and the only way to salvation.

Speak up when the time is right

Meanwhile, the people were waiting for Zechariah and wondering why he stayed so long in the temple. When he came out, he could not speak to them. They realized he had seen a vision in the temple, for he kept making signs to them but remained unable to speak. When his time of service was completed, he returned home. After this his wife Elizabeth became pregnant and for five months remained in seclusion. "The Lord has done this for me," she said. "In these days he has shown his favor and taken away my disgrace among the people. (Luke 1:21-24)

On the eighth day they came to circumcise the child, and they were going to name him after his father Zechariah, but his mother spoke up and said, "No! He is to be called John. (Luke 1:59-60)

While pregnant, Elizabeth was in seclusion for five months. It is unknown why she did this, but it could have been to meditate on the angel's prophecy and get prepared for what was to come. Or maybe she was waiting until she "showed more" so that people who doubted she was pregnant could see the evidence. This time of solitude was no doubt good for her.

Zechariah couldn't speak at all for the entire pregnancy. Eight days after the baby was born when it came time to name him everyone thought he would be named after Zechariah. But Elizabeth spoke up and said, "No! He is to be called John!" This probably got everyone talking and so they made signs to his father. This shows that he was not only dumb but possibly deaf as well. So Zechariah wrote out these words: "His name is John" (Luke 1:63). At that moment, he was finally able to speak and his first words were in praise of God and then he breaks out into some lengthy lyrics in Luke 1:67-80.

Elizabeth did not say much. Like Mary, possibly she kept many thoughts in her heart (Luke 2:19). But though a woman of few words, when the opportunity was made available, she spoke up and spoke out. She was not afraid to say what she knew to be true, no matter what others thought of her.

CHAPTER 12:

CHRISTMAS IS THE MOST WONDERFUL TIME OF THE YEAR

A GUY WAS on a game show and had to answer the question, "Name two of Santa's reindeer." "That's easy," he answered. "Rudolph and Olive." The host said, "We can accept Rudolph but explain Olive." "You know, Rudolph, the Red Nosed Reindeer – had a very shiny nose. And if you ever saw it, you would even say it glowed. Olive, the other reindeer…"

Christmas is a fun time of year. Decorations, gifts, special programs and parties all bring their own kind of excitement. But with all the activities surrounding the Christmas holiday, it is easy to miss the real meaning of Christmas – God became a man. This is referred to doctrinally as incarnation.

The incarnation is God, Creator of the universe, born as a baby. The God from whom all things come, became a human. Jesus, who was eternal, took on the form of the temporary, in order that temporary creations might gain eternal life. Jesus, who is one with the Father, endured separation from God so that those who were separated might become one with God. Jesus, who is truly God, came to be born in a flesh and blood body, born to a virgin, born in a stable, born in simplicity.

It is this truth that sets Christianity apart from all other religions of the world (including Judaism and Islam). It is unique to Christianity to discover a God who takes the initiative in becoming flesh in order to redeem sinful human beings. As C. S. Lewis aptly put it, "The Son of God became a man to enable men to become sons of God."

The incarnation makes for great Christmas carols and beautiful Christmas card covers. But what does it mean to the person who is scratching out a living by the skin of their teeth, who are not sure where the money for next week's groceries will come from? What does the incarnation mean to a young unmarried girl who just found out that she is pregnant and is scared to death to tell her parents? How does the incarnation help a nursing home resident who on the one hand does not want to be a burden on their family, but on the other hand hungers for the love of their children and grandchildren? Or what does the incarnation say to a person who has cancer, or AIDS, or who struggles with depression, or the gathering clouds of age, or even death? Does the incarnation have something to say to them? For them, Christmas doesn't seem to be a wonderful time of year. It just seems like any other day, maybe even worse because everyone else appears to be happy.

If Christmas does not have some help for those in need then it is just an excuse to express selfishness and greed. If it offers no hope, then Christmas is just an excuse for a party and a hangover. If Christmas does not speak to our needy situation, then it is just an excuse to forget the diet or take a vacation. The good news of Christmas is that we have more than Santa Claus, presents and lights.

So, why is Christmas such a wonderful time of year?

To answer this question, we turn to several Bible verses in 1 John. The Apostle John uses the words "appeared" or "manifested" to indicate the incarnation. These will give us a clue why it is so wonderful that Jesus came.

Jesus came to take away sins

And ye know that he was manifested to take away our sins; and in him is no sin. (1 John 3:5)

Sin is our biggest problem. Jesus came to solve that problem. God takes sin seriously, and so should we. In being "manifested," God identified with sinners. He "became flesh" (John 1:14). In His life, Jesus modeled perfect obedience to God, and in His death, He atoned for humankind's sin. The result of Christ's life, death, and resurrection is that God makes sinners holy when they trust Jesus Christ as their Savior.

A little boy went to the Washington Monument and told the guard, "I'd like to buy it." The guarded stooped down and asked how much do you have?" The boy responded that he had 34 cents. The guard looked at the boy and said, "You need to understand three things. First, 34 cents isn't enough. Even $34 million isn't enough. Second, it's not for sale. Third, if you are an American citizen, the Washington Monument already belongs to you." We, also, need to understand three things about God's forgiveness: First, we can't earn it. Second, it's not for sale. Third, if we accept Christ, we already have it.

The incarnation matters because it makes possible the forgiveness of our sins. The forgiveness of sin requires a sacrifice of blood (Hebrews 9:22). Blood comes only from real flesh and blood creatures. If Jesus were only divine, or like an angel, He would not be flesh and blood. Only because He took on human flesh could He be the sacrifice to atone for our sins. Had Jesus not taken on human flesh, our sins would not be forgiven. Because Jesus did take on human flesh, lived a sinless life (Hebrews 4:15) and offered His sinless life on the cross of Calvary, He can provide forgiveness, atonement, salvation and eternal life for us (Romans 5:1-21).

Christmas is a great time to surrender your life to Jesus and receive Him as personal Lord and Savior. Jesus came to us to save us. Consider going to Him to receive the greatest Christmas gift — forgiveness of sins.

Jesus came to destroy the works of the devil

He that committeth sin is of the devil; for the devil sinneth from the beginning. For this purpose the Son of God was manifested, that he might destroy the works of the devil. (1 John 3:8)

Satan is our worst enemy. He deceives us into sin and wants to destroy us. Jesus' arrival on planet Earth was a declaration of war on Satan. We must not underestimate the hostility and deceitfulness of the enemy of our soul. Jesus certainly did not.

Satan thought the cross was the end of Jesus; instead, it was the downfall of Satan's plan.

Harry Houdini, the famed escape artist, issued a challenge wherever he went. He could be locked in any jail cell and set himself free. He kept his promise, but one time something went wrong. He was placed in the cell, the door clanged shut. He took a piece of metal from his belt and began to try to pick the lock. For 30 minutes he worked. An hour passed, and he couldn't pick the lock. Finally, after two hours he collapsed in frustration, fell against the door, and it swung open. The door wasn't locked. The same is true for many Christians. The power of Satan has been destroyed, but he still has them locked in sin.

The origin of Satan is a mystery. Many believe he was once one of the highest angels, placed by God over the earth and over the other angels, and that he sinned against God and was cast down. Satan is not eternal, as is God, for he is a created being. He was not created sinful. His present nature is a result of his past rebellion. Satan is not like God. He is not all-powerful, all-knowing, or everywhere present. Satan is a rebel, but Christ is the obedient Son of God. Christ is God but was willing to become a servant. Satan was a servant and wanted to be like God.

"Destroy" from 1 John 3:8 does not mean 'annihilate.' It means 'to render inoperative, to rob of power.' Satan's power has been reduced and his weapons have been impaired. He is still a mighty foe, but he is no match for the power of God. Satan is a defeated enemy. He may still win a few battles here and there, but he has already lost the war! The sentence has been pronounced on him, but it will be a while before the punishment is delivered. A person who knows Christ, and who has been delivered from the bondage of sin through Christ's death on the cross, has no desire to obey Satan and live like a rebel.

Jesus came to show the love of God

In this was manifested the love of God toward us, because that God sent his only begotten Son into the world, that we might live through him. Herein is love, not that we loved God, but that he loved us, and sent his Son to be the propitiation for our sins. (1 John 4:9-10)

God's love is our best help. Christ coming to earth was an expression of God's love. How do we know God loves sinners? He sent His Son, Jesus. When we don't feel that God loves us, we need to look at objective truth. God reached out to us by sending the Son He loves, and the Son died for our sins and rose to give us an eternal relationship with God. 1 John 4:9-10 gives evidence that God truly loves us. First, God initiated the relationship (He sent His Son). Second, God gave His best (His only begotten Son). Third, God met our deepest needs (sin and God's wrath). A true story may help you understand the power of love.

Like any mother, when Karen found out that another baby was on the way, she did what she could to help 3-year-old Michael prepare for a new sibling. They found out that the new baby was going to be a girl, and day after day, night after night, Michael sang to his sister in mommy's tummy, building a bond of love with the baby before they even met her.

The pregnancy progressed normally for Karen. But serious complications arose during delivery. When Michael's little sister was finally born, she was in a very serious condition. An ambulance rushed the infant to the NIC unit at St. Mary's Hospital in Knoxville, Tennessee.

The days inched by, and the tiny baby grew worse. A pediatric specialist regretfully told Karen and her husband, 'There is very little hope. Be prepared for the worst." The parents contacted a local cemetery about a burial plot.

Little Michael, however, kept begging his parents to let him see his sister. "I want to sing to her," he said. But children were not allowed in intensive care. The second week in intensive care seemed to indicate a funeral by the end of the week. So Karen made up her mind. She would take Michael to see his sister, whether the hospital allowed it or not. If he didn't see her right away, he might never see his little sister alive.

As they walked in, the head nurse recognized him as a child and bellowed, "Get that kid out of here now! No children allowed." The mother instinct rose up strong in Karen, and the usually mild-mannered woman glared into the head nurse's face. "He is not leaving until he sings to his sister!"

Karen took him to the little baby's bedside. He gazed at his little sister losing her battle to live. After a moment, he began to sing. "You are my sunshine, my only sunshine, You make me happy when skies are gray."

Instantly, the baby began to respond. Her pulse rate calmed down and became more steady. "Keep singing, Michael." Karen encouraged.

"You'll never know, dear, how much I love you. Please don't take my sunshine away."

As Michael sang to his sister, the baby's staggered breathing became smoother. A healing was taking place.

The next day – the very next day – Michael's little sister was well enough to go home. *Women's Day* magazine called it "The Miracle of a Brother's Song." The medical staff just called it a miracle. Karen called it a miracle of God's love.

Jesus came to earth to sing a new song that would save us from death and make us a part of His family. What an incredible love He had for us – even before we were born! Christmas is the celebration of the most incredible love of all.

Christmas shows us how much God loves us. Christmas helps us understand true love. God wants His love for us to be shared with others.

CONCLUSION

DURING THE SEASON of shopping and entertaining, remember why Christmas is celebrated in the first place. We decorate our homes, send out cards, visit friends, buy presents, and go caroling. Some celebrate a portion of Christmas Day watching football games or going to a movie. For some, it's a time for drinking and partying. But this is a holiday to honor the fact that God sent His Son to be born in a manger and to become our Savior. As Christians, we should celebrate in a unique way. I'd like to suggest four responses to the birthday of Christ based on the people who were witnesses the first Christmas Day.

Celebrate Christmas by witnessing about Christ

And when they had seen it, they made known abroad the saying which was told them concerning this child. (Luke 2:17)

The shepherds "made known the saying which was told them concerning this child." We're to make Him known to those around us and help them understand that He came as a Savior. There are many opportunities available during Christmas. We can witness through the cards we send out. We witness by how we decorate our homes. We witness through the seasonal music we sing. And we witness by inviting people to attend church services with us. Many will come at this season of the year who would never darken our doors otherwise. Be intentional about sharing Christ this Christmas.

Celebrate Christmas by wondering at Christ

And all they that heard it wondered at those things which were told them by the shepherds. (Luke 2:18)

Those who heard the shepherds wondered at the things told them. There is a word we don't use much anymore — muse. It means sit back, meditate, and think. The word amuse adds the negative prefix which means "to not muse." Amusements are those things that keep us from thinking seriously about anything. Christmas is a wonderful time for amusement, yet when those in Luke 2 heard about Jesus they mused on Him. Think about it! Here is a story of purity wrapped up in the birth of a Child born to a young mother. Here is joy amidst seeming tragedy. Here is a great announcement to a lowly group of shepherds. Here is a baby born to die. Here is a king born in a stable to poor parents, yet was God manifest in flesh. G. Campbell Morgan wrote, "In the presence of such a holy miracle, there can be no fitting attitude of the human intellect save that of acceptance of the truth without any attempt to explain the mystery."

Celebrate Christmas by waiting before Christ

But Mary kept all these things, and pondered them in her heart. (Luke 2:19)

We also celebrate Christmas by waiting before Christ, even as Mary pondered all these things in her heart. You say, "Isn't that what you were just saying?" Well, the word ponder is even more intense than wonder. It means to delve beneath the surface and to contemplate, trying to understand. Mary pondered and treasured them up. She committed them to memory. She was a woman who thought deeply about what was happening in her life. It's easy to become so busy between Thanksgiving and Christmas that we don't spend time in personal Bible study and prayer. We can let the outward celebrations of the holiday take us away from the one thing that could mean the most to us as Christians. We have to make time for waiting before God.

Celebrate Christmas by worshiping Christ

And the shepherds returned, glorifying and praising God for all the things that they had heard and seen, as it was told unto them. (Luke 2:20)

The shepherds returned, glorifying and praising God. I believe Christmas affords tremendous opportunities for glorifying God as we sing our wonderful carols, as we pray personally, quietly praise Him, and publicly worship. To celebrate Christmas as Christians, we need to take a step back from the busyness of the season and the materialism of the world and focus on Him!

Years ago in a European country, a christening took place for a baby who had been born to royalty. As the guests arrived, a servant met them at the door and took their wraps. Eventually someone asked, "Where's the baby?" The nurse was sent to fetch him, but she couldn't find him. Finally, a guest recalled having seen the baby in the bed where the coats had been placed. The parents were horrified to find there the lifeless form of their son who had been smothered under the pile of coats. What irony. The real purpose of the gathering had been forgotten and the one to be honored was killed. I wonder if that isn't true for many at Christmas. Jesus is our celebration. He is our Honored One. He is our King. This Christmas honor Christ by witnessing, wondering, waiting before Him and worshiping Him!

ABOUT THE AUTHOR

Greg Burdine has been the senior pastor of Faith Baptist Church in Adrian, Michigan since 1994. He has been in pastoral ministry since 1982 and has served churches in Iowa, Ohio and Michigan. His passion is to help people understand and implement Biblical wisdom into their daily life. He has been married to his wife, Judy, since 1981 and has four grown children and seven grandchildren. Greg has an earned doctorate from Louisiana Baptist University. Beyond ministry, Greg loves to read, run and spend timewith his family.

Made in the USA
Lexington, KY
11 November 2019